To Ed —

Hope you enjoy the ride!

With all best wishes:

[signature]

June 13, 2010

LITTLE TRAINS TO FARAWAY PLACES

RAILROADS PAST AND PRESENT

George M. Smerk, editor

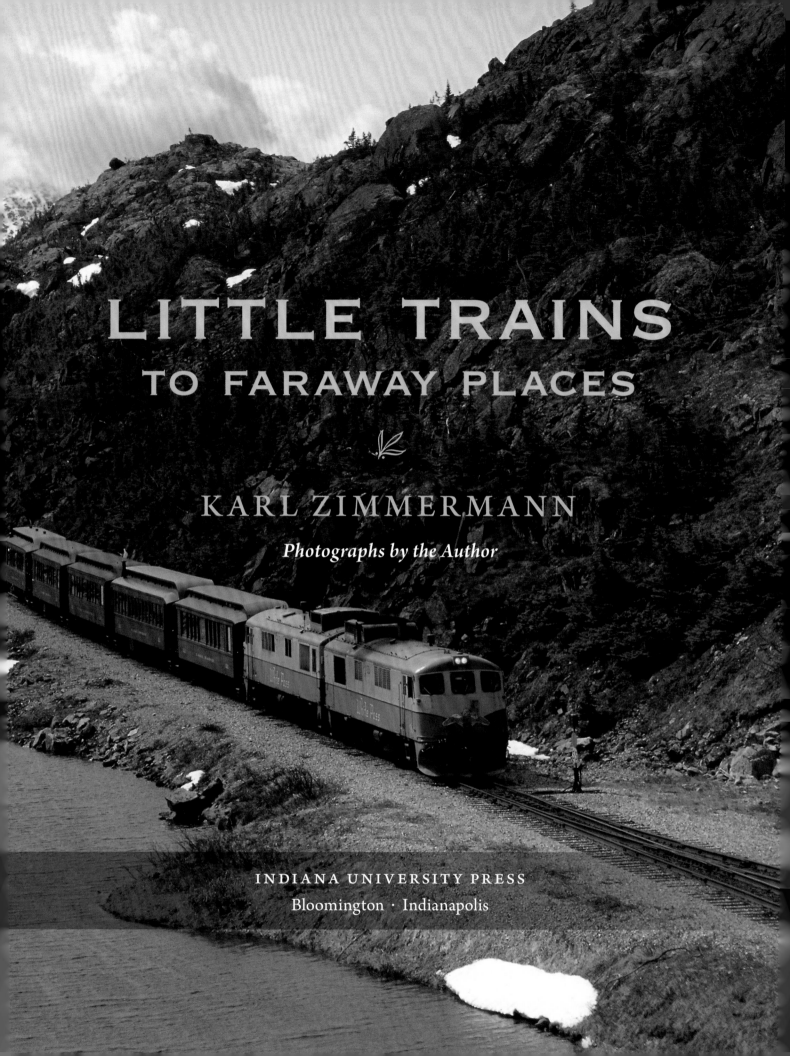

LITTLE TRAINS
TO FARAWAY PLACES

KARL ZIMMERMANN

Photographs by the Author

INDIANA UNIVERSITY PRESS
Bloomington · Indianapolis

This book is a publication of

Indiana University Press
601 North Morton Street
Bloomington, Indiana 47404-3797 USA

www.iupress.indiana.edu

Telephone orders   800-842-6796
Fax orders   812-855-7931
Orders by e-mail   iuporder@indiana.edu

∞ The paper used in this publication meets
the minimum requirements of the American National Standard for Information
Sciences—Permanence of Paper for Printed
Library Materials, ANSI Z39.48-1992.

Manufactured in China

Library of Congress Cataloging-in-
Publication Data

Zimmermann, Karl R.
  Little trains to faraway places /
Karl Zimmermann.
      p. cm. — (Railroads past and present)
  Includes bibliographical references
  and index.
  ISBN 978-0-253-35447-1 (cloth : alk.
paper) 1. Narrow gauge railroads.
2. Railroad passenger cars.
3. Railroad travel. I. Title.
  TF675.Z56 2010
  385.5'2—dc22
                          2009031621
  1 2 3 4 5 15 14 13 12 11 10

The Welshpool & Llanfair Light Railway's No. 14 steams toward Llanfair Caereinion. (PAGE I)
General Electric shovel-nose diesels on the White Pass & Yukon Route. (OVERLEAF)
Early morning in El Rancho in Guatemala. (FACING PAGE)
In Patagonia, Commodoro Py is a water stop on the Ferrocarril Industrial Rio Turbio. (PAGE VII)

THIS BOOK IS DEDICATED TO ALL MY FELLOW TRAVELERS
ON THE SLIM GAUGE, ESPECIALLY

Roger Cook, Rich Taylor, Rich Thom,
and—as always—Laurel

CONTENTS

Union Limited on the Porterville Branch in South Africa.

ACKNOWLEDGMENTS

This book has a number of godfathers, and it is my pleasure to thank them here. Part of each of the 17 chapters that follow has been in print before. Some chapters are products of a good deal of cutting and pasting, amplification, and revision, while others appear here very much as they were originally published.

Significantly more of these stories started in *Trains* magazine than in any other rail enthusiast publication, but *Passenger Train Journal, Railfan & Railroad, Locomotive & Railway Preservation,* and *International Railway Traveler* are all represented as well. So are a number of newspaper travel sections, especially those of the *Washington Post, Los Angeles Times, Globe & Mail, Sunday Star Ledger,* and *South Florida Sun-Sentinel.* In the course of seeing these pieces into print, I've worked with many fine editors at all these publications, but I single out one with pleasure and gratitude, Kevin P. Keefe, since it was on his watch at *Trains* (as assistant editor, editor, or publisher) and before that at *Passenger Train Journal* that a significant number of these stories appeared.

Any close reader of the chapters concerning my Latin American trips will recognize immediately that they were made possible by Chris Skow's Trains Unlimited, Tours. Although I traveled only once, to Patagonia, with Chris himself, Trains Unlimited was responsible for my getting to Ecuador, Guatemala, and Cuba as well, and my second trip to the White Pass & Yukon was occasioned by one of his company's photo charters. Skow was a veteran Latin American rail traveler and steam aficionado before he made it a business, and his good advice was the foundation on which I built my independent trip to the Teresa Cristina in Brazil. The opportunities Skow provided—to travel to sometimes difficult places and, through charter trains, experience railroading not otherwise available—was invaluable.

I've relied on the better memories (and sometimes better notes) of certain friends who traveled with me to the faraway places chronicled here. Their names are to be found in the most appropriate spot of all: on the dedication page. I'm deeply grateful for their support and friendship.

The *Blue Train* dining car.

Talyllyn Railway in Wales. (FACING PAGE)

LITTLE TRAINS TO FARAWAY PLACES

A Guayaquil & Quito train climbs the switchbacks
on the Devil's Nose in Ecuador. (ABOVE)

Waiter in the tiny dining car of the Esquel Branch mixed train,
which Paul Theroux dubbed the "Old Patagonian Express." (BELOW)

INTRODUCTION · THE LURE OF THE NARROW GAUGE

THE MYSTIQUE OF THE NARROW-GAUGE RAILROAD IS powerful, complex, and undeniable. From the Colorado Rockies to the Harz Mountains of Germany, from Switzerland to Patagonia, from Australia to South Africa, these little lines have held a special kind of magic.

A waiter in a powder blue jacket serves steak in the diminutive dining car of the "Old Patagonian Express" as its ancient locomotive chuffs up-grade. A steam-powered rotary plow hurls snow into the blue Colorado sky. Viewed from a boxcar roof, Ecuador's "Devil's Nose," a cone-shaped mountain of precipitous stone, looms ahead; the switchbacks that scale it look imposing, if not impossible. In late spring, Bernina Pass on Switzerland's Rhaetian Railway seems both the end and the top of the world, dazzling with remnant snow and the water of glaciers. Aboard South Africa's *Blue Train,* the view is through glass tinted with gold dust, and the living is high.

Why the magic? For openers, there's the inherent charm of diminution. Indeed, some narrow-gauge railroads are downright Lilliputian. They're by no means toys, however; each was built smaller than standard in dead earnest, for a particular reason. Almost always, that reason was economy, since narrow-gauge lines are cheaper than standard-gauge to build and oper-ate. The wilder the terrain, the greater the economy, because tunnels, cuts, and mountainside ledges are proportionally smaller for narrow-gauge track, and grades can be steeper. This all means that narrow-gauge lines often run through rugged, remote, beautiful country, which is yet another reason for their charm. One more reason, a related one, is the sense of can-do, make-do, and the marginal. Every narrow-gauge line is by definition a compromise. Many had the cards stacked against them right from the time of their creation, so often they have been heroic in survival, noble even in defeat. And profoundly human. Since the narrow gauges rarely merited heavy investment in modernization, in many cases the old ways lingered on, and the old ways generally involved doing things manually.

Perhaps the most notable survivor was the steam locomotive, often saved by a railroad's lack of funds to dieselize. In the case of Pennsylvania's East Broad Top and Colorado's Denver & Rio Grande Western, both the railroad and the locomotives survived long enough through benign neglect to enter conscious preservation, which occurred in 1960 for the EBT and 1970 for the D&RGW. The same thing happened decades later in the Harz Mountains of former East Germany and in Argentina's Patagonia. Indeed, many of the narrow-gauge stories that follow are steam stories, and more than a few are preservation stories.

Certainly narrow-gauge railroading conjures images of marginal track, wooden coaches, and antique steam locomotives. On the other hand, consider South Africa's *Blue Train* and Australia's *Queenslander.* Both are built in the "Cape Gauge," 42 inches, that is often found where the British Empire extended. Both trains were extraordinarily glamorous and comfortable. And the electrified network of meter-gauge mountain railways in Switzerland runs with the precision of a Swiss watch. I've chosen to be a strict constructionist, and since these trains undeniably run on tracks narrower than standard gauge, they're in the book.

Consider the chapters that follow my "life list," to borrow a term from the bird watchers, a group of enthusiasts every bit as intense as the train-watching (and riding) fraternity. There are, of course, many hundreds of narrow-gauge lines that I've not seen and that thus are not to be found between these covers. While many of them have vanished (not necessarily without a trace, happily), there are survivors that I hope to discover in the future. However, from any life list there are bound to be painful omissions, and there certainly are such blanks on my narrow-gauge list. Like all of my generation, I've encountered the iconic Maine 2-footers only in preservation and, in my case, only glancingly, at Edaville amid the cranberry bogs of Massachusetts and, later, in Portland, Maine. Furthermore, no one could be such a devotee of the Colorado narrow-gauge lines as I and not lament missing the Rio Grande Southern. If I could be a time-traveler, Maine and Colorado would surely be among my first destinations.

On the Denver & Rio Grande Western, this iconic sign once
announced the end of the dual-gauge track from Alamosa. Today
it stands proudly on the Cumbres & Toltec Scenic Railroad.

The most painful and troublesome omission from my life list, and thus
from this book, is India's Darjeeling Himalayan Railway, the "Toy Train," perhaps the most photogenic, atmospheric, internationally famous slim-gauge
line of all and a UNESCO World Heritage Site to boot. You could argue that
this line is the quintessence of narrow gauge. It still tops my wish list, but
substantial diesel incursion has now occurred, and distance suggests that it
may never move from wish list to life list.

I was not born an enthusiast of the narrow gauge, nor did little railways
first catch my fancy as a teenager. In fact, I was initially drawn, in 1960, to Durango and the Denver & Rio Grande Western, my first narrow-gauge railroad,
simply because of the steam locomotives. The standard-gauge steam power
of the Pennsylvania Railroad, Norfolk & Western, Canadian National, and
Canadian Pacific—my earliest railfan passions and photographic quarry—
had recently vanished, and I sought a replacement. After hulking brawlers like
the N&W's Y-6 articulateds and elegant speedsters like CPR Royal Hudsons,
the Rio Grande's outside-frame Mikados seemed a trifle slow and undersized.
But the narrow-gauge bug bit and bit hard, and D&RGW's little trains became
the (often unrequited) railway love of my life.

Narrow gauge is in and of itself a slippery concept, subject to multiple interpretations. Historically, railroads have been built to dozens of gauge measurements, and in a good number of them significant track mileage was constructed. "Standard" is a term universally agreed upon today, and those measurements on the two sides of the curious 4 feet 8½ inches that evolved as "standard" are understood to be "broad" or "narrow." There is no magic to any particular number; rails distanced anywhere from the roughly 7 feet of Isambard Kingdom Brunel's Great Western Railway in Britain (opened in 1838 and completely converted to standard gauge by 1892) to the 15 inches of the miniature but very much workaday Romney, Hythe & Dymchurch, also in Britain, have gotten the job done.

How the curious, odd width of 4 feet 8½ inches came to dominate the world's railroads is a conundrum to which there's been an almost universal answer: that this was the width between Roman chariot wheels. Once ruts had been worn into primitive roads, the theory goes, vehicles were replicated in this gauge so they would ride easily in these ruts. The gauge spread to Britain during the Roman occupation, where it later was adopted for the primitive colliery railroads. From here on the story is documented: George Stephenson, the most influential of early railway engineers, designer of steam locomotives *Locomotion* and *Rocket,* chose it for his pioneering Stockton & Darlington Railway, which opened in 1825. In 1846, the British Parliament gave 4 feet 8½ inches the official imprimatur by passing the Gauge Act. Many scholars doubt "the chariot" derivation but without positing an alternative explanation. For me personally, seeing firsthand the ruts of chariot wheels worn into a stone roadway at the ruins in Ephesus lent some credibility to what had previously seemed entirely far-fetched.

Broad gauge was once a factor in the United States; the Erie Railroad's (until 1880) 6-foot and the 5-foot of many lines in the South, both before and after the Civil War, are a few of the better-known examples. In time, the huge advantage of interchange of rolling stock (a factor the South discovered to its chagrin during the war) led to standardization. In 1863, Congress ruled that 4 feet 8½ inches would be the gauge for the new transcontinental line, and the die was cast.

Internationally, broad gauge is very much alive. "Irish Gauge," 5 feet 3 inches, remains the norm in its homeland and has migrated to Brazil and Australia, the preeminent land of multiple gauges. "Indian Gauge" is 5 feet 6 inches. "Iberian Gauge" of 5 feet 5⅔ inches still blankets Spain and Portugal. "Russian Gauge" of 4 feet 11⅚ inches, the norm throughout he former Soviet Union, was established in 1842 when Tsar Nicholas II hired American railway engineer George Washington Whistler to build Russia's first major railway, between Moscow and St. Petersburg. (G. W. Whistler was the father of artist James McNeill Whistler.) The tsar's choice of broad gauge, creating

Taking water at Mayrhofen, the end of
the line, on Austria's Zillertalbahn.

a "break of gauge" with Europe's standard gauge, has often been reported as
strategic, making invasion more difficult. Gauge multiplicity still prevailed
in 1842, however, so this explanation may well be an intriguing canard—in
the category, some would say, of chariot wheels.

Standard, broad, and narrow: it's all relative, really, and throughout southern Africa (and in other places within Britain's colonial reach) 3-foot 6-inch-
gauge, "Cape Gauge," was and is "standard." Watching, for instance, one of
South African Railways' burly 25-class 4-8-4's roar down the arrow-straight

main line across the vast, empty, semi-desert Karoo in 1977, it was hard for me to get my head around the idea of South African Railways' being narrow gauge. But, in fact, it was and is, and this diminution makes all the more remarkable, for instance, the *Blue Train*'s spacious luxury and the prowess of the odd-looking Beyer-Garratts and other steam locomotives that still roamed South Africa when I first visited.

Not every narrow-gauge railway on my life list gets a chapter in this book, for reasons more arbitrary than profound. In some cases, I simply didn't feel I had a good enough story to tell—which is different from saying the railroad wasn't worth telling about. In France, I managed to ride only the lower two-thirds of 94-mile meter-gauge Chemins de Fer de Provence from Nice to Digne, high in the French Alps. The railcars were humble but comfortable, with broad windows and high-backed plush seats. Someday I may go back and finish the route.

Joining the main line of the Austrian Federal Railways at Jenbach are a pair of steam-powered (at least sometimes) narrow-gauge lines that I visited briefly in May 1999. The meter-gauge, rack-and-pinion Achenseebahn, opened in 1889, climbs 4.21 miles to Lake Achen, while the 2-foot 6-inch-gauge Zillertalbahn, just over a decade younger, runs (with steam or diesel) in another direction, to Mayrhofen. A return visit is in order—as is one to our own great cogwheel line, New Hampshire's Mount Washington Cog Railway, 55-inch-gauge and thus just narrower than standard. It opened in 1869, making the Achenseebahn look young.

The Ferrocarril Industrial Rio Turbo runs straight as an arrow
through the vast emptiness of Patagonia. (ABOVE)

On the East Broad Top, Mikado No. 12 moves its train toward the station-general
offices building at Orbisonia. A Baldwin sister waits in front of the depot. (FACING)

Thinking about Mount Washington raises the question of "faraway places." It isn't one, of course, since I grew up in New Jersey and live there now. Nor, I suppose, is Colorado, but the old Rio Grande narrow-gauge lines are just too flat-out wonderful to omit, and I've never stood at Cumbres Pass and not felt I was somewhere removed, in time as well as space. Pennsylvania's East Broad Top, another favorite of mine, nearly made it into the book, but the fact that only a small section of its original route is in operation weighed against it.

The stories that follow are more various than similar. Some focus on scenery, some on history, some on equipment, others on people—though all chapters embrace the full spectrum of these to some extent. Taken together, this smorgasbord, this life list, is a composite slim-gauge personal journey and a punched ticket to ride along.

The *Glacier Express* is dropping down a steep rack-and-
pinion-assisted grade into
Andermatt. The restaurant
car at the end of the train
will be dropped there before
the rest of the consist con-
tinues on to Brig. (ABOVE)

From the restaurant car on
the *Glacier Express,* Andermatt looks like a model
village, spread out across
the valley below. (LEFT)

SWITZERLAND'S LEISURELY EXPRESSES

THE VALLEY OF THE UPPER RHONE IN SOUTHEASTERN Switzerland had been broad, green, and fertile for the roughly 25 miles we'd traveled from the railway-junction town of Brig. Now, as our little train reached Oberwald, the mountains began to close in dramatically. Laurel and I were with Jennifer and Emily, our then-young daughters, aboard the *Glacier Express* on the rails of the Furka-Oberalp, one of the three independent meter-gauge railways that (at the time) operated this summer-only tourist-toting train between Zermatt and St. Moritz, Switzerland's quintessentially luxe resorts.

Like virtually all Swiss railways, these three lines were electrified. The Furka-Oberalp was a mixed rack-and-pinion (cogwheel) and adhesion line, and our locomotive, No. 33, slowed to engage the rack rail. The 33, a B-B (indicating two four-wheel trucks) box cab, dated from 1941 and thus was on hand when electrification was inaugurated on the FO. We were in for a stiff climb through a spiral tunnel to the town of Gletsch—"glacier" in German, and we were riding through the German-speaking region of this tiny but diverse country, where no fewer than four languages are spoken.

It was summer, July 1977, but we were growing chilly as we climbed. Still, I was leaning out through the broad window of our coach, craning my neck to glimpse the spectacle I knew lay ahead: the Rhone Glacier. Suddenly there it was—a mass of azure ice, incredible even at a distance; from it gushed the unending freshet of ice-melt that forms the headwaters of the Rhone River. At 11:43, exactly on time, the train that takes its name from the Rhone Glacier eased to a stop at Gletsch, a town which does, too.

The eastbound journey of the *Glacier Express* had begun three hours earlier, at 8:44 AM, at Zermatt. This resort at the foot of a soaring, iconic tor, the 14,693-foot Matterhorn, banned automobiles then—and still does. Passengers who had stayed overnight amid the elegance of the Zermatterhof, the city's classic Old World hotel, might have arrived at the chalet-style railway station in a trim blue carriage lettered for that hotel, pulled by a matched pair of dappled horses and attended by a liveried coachman and a footman in tails. The *Glacier Express,* waiting there on the tracks of the Brig-Visp-Zermatt Railway, was a modern and comfortable conveyance, yet one with ties to an era when horse-drawn travel had been much less of an anomaly than it was when we visited Zermatt.

At the head of the *Glacier Express* was a B-B electric locomotive of steeple-cab design, one of six delivered beginning in August 1929 to open the electrification on what was then the Visp-Zermatt Railway. Though very different in appearance, these VZ locomotives in fact were the mechanical and electrical prototypes for the Furka-Oberalp box cabs that were built a dozen years later. The steeple-cab and four trailing coaches were bright red, a livery all BVZ and FO motive power and rolling stock shared— the commonality a result, no doubt, of the operating partnership that existed between those lines from 1925 to 1960. (On January 1, 2003, the BVZ and FO would merge to form the Matterhorn Gotthard Railway.) Actually, the distinction on these railroads between motive power and rolling stock was blurred, since paired electric motor coaches—and, in the case of FO, motorized baggage cars—often served in place of locomotives. Affixed to the sides of the red coaches, below the windows, metal destination signs read "Glacier Express"; on some the bottom line was Chur, on others, St. Moritz.

The descent from Zermatt was through the narrow valley of the Matter Visp River, with towering mountains impinging and limiting the scope of vistas. There were four rack-and-pinion stretches on the BVZ, where cogwheels engaged a ladderlike center rail allowing locomotives or motor cars to hoist themselves up (or drop safely down) the grade. One of these was through Kipfen Gorge, with its foaming, tumbling staircase of waterfalls. At Visp, for a time the railway's northern terminus and the location of its shops, the BVZ entered the spacious valley of the Rhone and turned sharply eastward

In 1977, all the windows on the *Glacier Express's* cars, including this Furka Oberalp second-class coach, opened to the fresh Alpine air.

to follow that river upstream into Brig, paralleling the standard-gauge main line from Lausanne of the Swiss Federal Railways—variously Schweizerische Bundesbahnen (SBB) in German, Chemins de fer fédéraux suisses (CFF) in French, and Ferrovie federali svizzere (FFS) in Italian.

This 5.5-mile extension, which turned the VZ into the BVZ, was completed in 1930 and was the final link in the 168-mile through route from Zermatt to St. Moritz. It made possible the *Glacier Express,* which was inaugurated the following year. Across the Rhone Valley from the BVZ, high on the mountainside, the brown locomotives of the Bern-Lötschberg-Simplon, an independent standard-gauge carrier, sped trains between Brig and Bern to the north.

Brig was the perfect showcase for the corporate diversity of Swiss railroads, which made them unique among European rail systems. Since it was a crossroads of rail commerce, Brig offered a smorgasbord of delights to the rider and watcher of trains—me. To the southeast ran the SBB line through the Simplon Tunnel to Domodossala and Milano in Italy. Northeastward, the FO extended to Andermatt and Disentis, where it connected with the Rhätische Bahn, or Rhaetian Railway, then the third partner in the *Glacier Express* operation and Europe's most extensive meter-gauge railway. To the west were the busy lines of the SBB, BLS, and BVZ.

My family and I lodged in Brig at the Hotel Victoria. The best part about our fourth-floor corner room was its balcony, from which we could view the entire rail show. Across the way stood the imposing, multitrack, standard-gauge SBB/BLS station, which seemed never to lack activity. Directly below our balcony, in the middle of the street on which both the hotel and the mainline station fronted, was the stub-end terminal of the BVZ and the FO. Beyond its platforms were the Furka-Oberalp motor shed and coach yard and, further back, the Brig-Visp-Zermatt facilities. A tiny FO electric switcher, the Toonerville Trolley of freight motors, shuttled about, working the passenger station and freight interchange tracks. Not much more than a pantograph-topped shed on a square platform, this little beast reminded me that within the imposing carbodies of most electric locomotives is a great deal of empty space. BVZ had a pair of diminutive diesels, just as unassuming as the FO's motor, to handle the switching at Visp and Zermatt.

From our balcony I'd watched the electric switcher and its confreres in red: a BVZ steeple cab arriving with a mixed train, motor-coach pairs pulling to the platform to load, a light FO box cab humming in from the motor shed to get on its train. At 10:13 AM, the *Glacier Express* swung into view from the BVZ main, slipped through the throat of the small yard, and stopped at the south side of the platform. Just a dozen minutes later it had received some extra coaches, exchanged its BVZ steeple cab for an FO box cab, and was on its way out of town, heading up the Rhone Valley to Gletsch.

The day we rode the *Glacier Express* through Gletsch was invigoratingly cold but brilliantly sunny. While the train was stopped there, almost everyone in our first-class coach—identifiable at a glance from outside by the yellow stripe running just below the roof line—donned coats. The train began to climb again, zigzagging up the wall of the still-narrowing valley with rack-and-pinion assist. This brought us close to the glacier, *die Gletsch,* an extraordinary valley full of frosted blue, flat-topped, rock-bottomed ice. Snow was suddenly all around, bright in the sun's glare, until we were plunged into the blackness of 1.25-mile Furka Tunnel, where we crested the pass at 7,088 feet, a climb of 4,883 feet from Brig.

A few minutes later we emerged on the other side of the tunnel into a vastly different world. In place of the bright sun was a shrouding of clouds and mist. As we began the rack-assisted descent through a deserted valley, we looked back toward the tunnel portal, surrounded by broad swatches of snow on the soft green fabric of the mountainside. The low-hanging clouds shut us off from everything but the verdant hills, dotted with alpine wildflowers and grazing cows. Our small red train seemed an unlikely visitor, interrupting an almost eerie stillness. Even more unlikely was the bridge over the Steffenbach Gorge that we soon crossed. This rather ordinary-looking span was actually extraordinary, for it was designed to be dismantled each winter to prevent its destruction by the massive avalanches that ran through the gorge. Just one day was required in the fall to collapse this hinged wonder in upon its abutments and only two days to erect it again in the spring.

Soon we reached Andermatt, a summer and winter resort town nestled in the Urseren Valley. Just seven minutes station time was sufficient to allow a diminutive electric switcher to cut in the Rhätische Bahn's ex-Mitropa restaurant car that would serve lunch on into Chur, one of two eastern endpoints for the *Glacier Express.* (Mitropa, operator of sleeping and dining cars, primarily in parts of Germany, Austria, and Hungary, had gotten its start during World War I because the dominant, Belgium-based Wagons-Lits company belonged to the enemy. The name Mitropa is a compression of *Mitteleuropa,* or Middle Europe.)

The tiny locomotive, a "box" cab in the most literal sense of the word, dated from 1917. That year, its original owner, the Schöllenen Railway, opened its 2.3-mile meter-gauge rack-and-pinion line from Andermatt down the wild Schöllenen Gorge to Göschenen, at the north end of the Gotthard Tunnel on the Swiss Federal Railway's busiest north-south artery. The Schöllenen Bahn is short but spectacular, running for much of its brief way in tunnels or snow sheds, *galleries pare-avalanches,* and crossing the River Reuss twice, once over a great, coursing waterfall. It's also strategically important, linking the FO with the SBB to Luzern, Zürich, and Locarno, as well as major cities in Germany, Italy, and beyond. For this reason the FO acquired the SchB in 1961. Since then, red FO motor coaches had shuttled back and forth between Göschenen and Andermatt, leaving the tiny and elderly box cabs (which had been rebuilt in 1941) to handle an occasional extra train as well as the switching at Andermatt.

As soon as the restaurant car—a 1929–30 veteran—was tacked onto the consist of the *Glacier Express,* a mad rush ensued for its 24 seats. We had reserved for the first sitting and were relieved to see the name "Zimmermann" on a table when we were carried into the car by a surge of hungry people. In contrast to practically everything else about the three sparkling railroads that hosted the *Glacier Express,* the restaurant car had a comfortable patina of age. It was wood-paneled, broad-windowed, not air-conditioned—and small. The diminution extended to the kitchen, a cubbyhole that turned out meals of remarkable quality.

As was the custom of Schweizerische Speisewagon-Gesellschaft—the Swiss Dining-car Company, which operated the car—the menu for the noon meal was a set, *table d'hôte carte,* offering no choices. Anything else would have placed impossible demands on the tiny galley and would have taken too long to serve anyway. Our meal was an excellent *escallope de veau au beurre* with a commendable salad, preceded by onion soup and followed by a cheese board and pear compote, all accompanied, appropriately, by a bottle of Côte du Rhone, which had been waiting on our table when we sat down. Alas, service was a tad rushed, even careless, no doubt because there was a second sitting to follow. But the food was tasty, and who'd want to miss the chance to lunch aboard what may have been the only dining car operating anywhere in the world on a cogwheel railway?

Leaving Andermatt, we climbed immediately on a rack section, criss-crossing the hillside above town in wide loops on successively higher levels until we reached a commanding prospect, the ideal way to say farewell to the alpine gem of a village now far below, looking as if it belonged on a model railroad. The grade was 11 percent there, so stiff that the soup dishes slid on their saucers, and we were glad that our now-open bottle of wine was held in a restraining ring, which folded down from the window sill for that purpose. Where else could rail-bound travelers enjoy a full meal with the grind and clatter of rack and pinion in their ears? (Souvenir glasses with slanted stems, supposedly to keep the wine from spilling on the steep grades, that are sold aboard the diners were and are more fun than functional.)

The climb continued until we skirted Oberalp Lake, traveling in an avalanche gallery for much of its length, then went over the top at Oberalppasshöne, the second pass yielding the name Furka-Oberalp for the railway, this one a mere 6,670 feet, 1,960 feet above Andermatt. From there we dropped down a steep rack-assisted section before easing on into Disentis. Considering the altitude gained and lost and the many miles of rack-and-pinion running, it is no reflection on the FO's handing of the *Glacier Express* that we have been averaging only about 18 miles an hour.

At Disentis, BVZ and FO red yielded to Rhätische Bahn green. The mode of operation changed, too, when the *Glacier Express* was handed over to RhB for the completion of its journey to Chur or St. Moritz. The Rhaetian Railway—243 miles long at that time (and longer now, truly a system, with a multiplicity of lines, unlike the simple point-to-point BVZ and FO)—eschews rack and pinion, so running is somewhat faster. The *Glacier Express* will average, for instance, 33 miles per hour from Disentis into Chur. But while it climbs its grades by adhesion only, this in no way should suggest inferior scenery or less spectacular engineering.

In fact, the need to keep grades at a maximum of 4.5 percent on the RhB has arguably created the most interesting and brilliantly engineered route of all. It featured 498 bridges for a total length of 8 miles and 118 tunnels and avalanche galleries, plunging RhB trains into 24 miles of darkness. Yet its mainline style of operation made the Rhaetian Railway seem a slightly miniature version of the mostly standard-gauge Swiss Federal Railways. That RhB and SBB both painted their equipment in green reinforced this; even the rich chocolate brown that RhB used on its older locomotives echoed a by-then-outmoded part of SBB heritage.

It's a sunny afternoon in July 1977, and the
Glacier Express has just arrived in Zermatt.

When we left Disentis, bound east toward Chur, up ahead were three
additional coaches and a baggage car, all green, and a 1,600-horsepower B-B
locomotive, one of 10 delivered in 1947 and 1953 to begin the modern motive-
power era on RhB. Numbered 601–610, the motors were the railroad's first
to wear green and be given names, traditions that were carried on with the
impressive B-B-B articulated locomotives, 701–707, delivered in 1958 and
1965, and on Nos. 611–620, the 2,200-horsepower B-B thyristor-equipped
electrics of 1973. (The thyristor converted the railway's alternating current
to direct current.)

At Reichenau-Tamins, the *Glacier Express* split, part continuing east over
RhB's only double track for the 6 miles to Chur (capital of the Canton of
the Grisons, where the language, one of four in Switzerland, is Latin-linked
Romansh). Our section undertook the more substantial 49-mile trek south
to St. Moritz. This led us over the Albula Line, as spectacular as anything
we had seen so far. Before long we crossed the leggy, graceful, curved Land-
wasser Viaduct—a handsome, Starrucca-like stone structure 427 feet long
and 213 feet high—then plunged into a tunnel through the cliff that formed
the bridge's eastern support. This iconic location, probably the most famous
on the RhB, has graced many a travel poster.

A Swiss art critic, Iso Camartin, wrote of the experience: "A ride on the
Rhaetian Railway through the valley of Albulatal to Engadin and onward
over the Bernina Pass to the south could easily lead you to believe that the
wonderful natural landscape was somehow incomplete until people of intel-
ligence and foresight decided to build a railway line through this land of steep
slopes to make its beauty absolute." In 2008, the Abula and Bernina lines of
RhB would be designated a UNESCO World Heritage Site.

Emerging from the tunnel, we approached Filisur, the junction with the
Davos line—the original Rhaetian Railway main, which makes a northerly

circle up to Davos (a spa there was RhB's original destination), Klosters, and finally Lanquart, the home of the RhB shops, just 9 miles north of Chur. At Filisur, we saw No. 412, one of RhB's gutty looking jackshaft-driven locomotives that were smaller versions of Swiss Federal Railways' famous articulated "Crocodiles"—"Krokodils" in German, a nickname conferred by rail enthusiasts.

Fifteen of these RhB 1,200-horsepower motors, originally required by the heavy trains and long grades of the Albula Line, were delivered by Brown, Bovari & Company, in tandem with Schweizerische Lokomotivfabrik Winterthur, through the 1920s. We saw those side-rodded "baby crocodiles" on passenger, goods, and mixed trains—such as the Davos-Filisur turn, No. 412's assignment. The "Krok" had twin protruding headlights reminiscent of eyes. Low hoods fore and aft could be imagined as snout and tail, and the whirling crankshafts and flapping rods made the beast appear, at least to the imaginative and whimsical, to be crawling. In shiny brown paint, with numerals and railway identification in gleaming brass, this locomotive was a fetching sight. I fell in love on the spot.

Beyond Filisur, we encountered a yet more astonishing stretch of the Albula Line: the 8 railway miles between Bergün and Preda, just 3.75 miles as the crow flies, in which the tracks climb 1,365 feet. Two elbow tunnels—Plaz and God—and three spiral tunnels—Rugnux, Toua, and Zuondra—helped hold the grade to 3.5 percent, very doable for electric-powered adhesion locomotives. At Samedan we stopped. Here trains split for Pontresina and the RhB's Bernina Line to Tirano, just into Italy, and for St. Moritz. Switching the yard by the station was box cab No. 221, a chocolate-colored veteran constructed in 1913 and rebuilt in 1945. Electric locomotives have a long shelf life.

When the *Glacier Express* pulled out, glamorous St. Moritz was just a few miles ahead on the Upper Engadin, a high plateau 25 miles long and 5,900 feet above sea level. We detrained there at 5:15 PM, eight and a half hours, a mere 138 miles, and countless scenic marvels from Zermatt. We had seen the Matterhorn, among Europe's most famous peaks, and followed the Rhone and the Rhein, two of its great rivers. We had crested mountain passes and crossed stone viaducts. Most appropriately of all, we had rubbed shoulders with a glacier.

Switzerland was far too wonderful for me not to return, and I did on a number of occasions—but not for a long while. Tour guide and author George Drury described the country as "a theme park for the railfan," which I thought summed it up perfectly. However, my next visit didn't come until September 1994, when I passed through on a journey by train, tram, ship, and boat from Russia's St. Petersburg to Switzerland's Rothorn Kulm. This was a weeklong trek that involved 26 rail and water conveyances, including the

By 1999 the *Glacier Express* has acquired a panorama car, fourth back from the locomotive, and the restaurant car (the first in the train) has been franchised to Gourmino and wears a blue dress. (ABOVE)

One of RhB's distinctive "baby Kroks" heads a Kalmbach charter. (BELOW)

Harzer Schmalspurbahnen (see chapter 9), but nary a rubber-tired vehicle. I traveled on the modernistic, high-tech *Crystal Panoramic Express* on the Montreux-Oberland Bernois and behind a rack-and-pinion steam locomotive—itself oddly high-tech, built in 1992—on the Brienzer Rothorn Bahn (see chapter 10).

When I finally got back to the Rhaetian Railway and had the chance to ride the Bernina line south into Italy, a route that had beckoned on my first trip 22 years earlier, I was with a group. It was May 1999, and I was one of the leaders of a tour organized by Kalmbach Publishing Company for readers of its various train-related magazines. The intervening 22 years had, of course, brought lots of changes. The essence of the RhB survived intact, although its green locomotives and coaches had morphed to red. The charismatic little chocolate-colored "baby crocodiles" were gone from regular service, although the railroad had retained a few for charters, and our group enjoyed a short outing behind one—from the railroad's headquarters at Landquart to Chur, aboard basic but historic four-wheel coaches.

The *Glacier Express* had gained "Panorama Cars," sort of single-level domes, which I actually found rather cramped, even claustrophobic, compared with standard coaches with windows that opened. The ancient dining cars survived, now franchised as Gourmino and wearing a distinctive blue livery—and perhaps more "ye olde" than when I first encountered them; then their antiquity had just happened and wasn't yet a "theme." On the FO, the collapsible bridge was gone, made unnecessary in 1982 by a line rerouting through the new 9.6-mile-long Furka Base Tunnel, which bypassed the avalanche area. This allowed the *Glacier Express* to become a year-round train—busiest now, in fact, in ski season, serving as it does Switzerland's preeminent ski resorts.

The Rhaetian Railway comprises a number of routes, all scenic: the Albula, the Bernina, the Engadine, the Davos, the Arosa, the Bünder Oberland. Our tour group rode most of these routes. In running from Chur to Tirano, just across the border into Italy, the *Bernina Express* duplicates some of the most spectacular parts of the *Glacier Express*'s route, but there were stunning sections I'd never ridden before. At Bernina Pass, said to be the only crossing of the Alps made above ground, we ran along the shore of Lago Bianca—"White Lake," chalky with "glacier milk." Here the landscape was starkly, fiercely beautiful.

From there the rails zigzagged down a series of switchbacks into a lush Mediterranean-seeming valley, a landscape hugely different from the Alpine otherworldliness of the pass. This welcoming, comfortable countryside was the setting for another engineering gem, the circular Brusio Viaduct, which our train rounded in a tight spiral before splitting one of the arches and heading on to Tirano, just over the border into Italy.

The Rhaetian Railway's *Bernina Express* along Lago Bianco.

"It's like a model train set!" exclaimed one of our tour group, likely a modeler himself.

I've one last story to tell about the Rhaetian Railway. Aboard the *Bernina Express* on the way down to Tirano, we floated the idea that, in order to see more of the railroad, the group might enjoy looping back to Chur by the long, circuitous way, via Davos and Landquart, rather than returning on the Albula line, the direct way we'd come. Some members would, some wouldn't. At Tirano, I asked the stationmaster if our charter coach could be cut off at Filisur and travel the "back road." After a minute or two on the telephone, he had that move approved and organized, even though the car would have to be switched an additional time at Davos. This ready flexibility astonished me.

"Everything runs like clockwork," an equally impressed passenger said to me. And indeed it did. Not long afterward we were again aboard our coach. The huge, imperious gong that announces train arrivals and departures began to ring, melodiously but urgently. The stationmaster appeared and raised his magic wand, the paddle with the green disk on the end, and we were off—accelerating rapidly, another adventure at hand.

The Lake Bennett excursion train waits on the dock at Skagway for passengers disembarking from the *Princess Patricia* to board.

2

NARROW AND NORTHERLY
THE WHITE PASS & YUKON

TO BOARD OUR EXCURSION TRAIN ON THE 3-FOOT-GAUGE White Pass & Yukon Route, our family didn't have far to walk: just down a ship's steep gangway and a few steps across a wood-planked pier.

It was June 28, 1978, my first visit to Skagway, the port city on Alaska's panhandle at the head of the Inside Passage. The WP&Y was definitely a side dish on this journey, not the main course, which was the classic little ship that brought us to Skagway. The railroad was so delectable, though, that I knew I'd eventually have to go back for a second helping—which I did, though not until decades had passed.

Laurel, Jennifer, Emily, and I arrived in Skagway by sea from Vancouver, as generations of travelers had before us, along with countless shiploads of cargo. Our vessel was the *T.E.V. Princess Patricia,* a tiny gem of a ship that itself had railroad lineage, belonging to Canadian Pacific. T.E.V. stood for "turbine electric vessel," and the turbines of this 6,062-ton ship were powered by steam. Along with sister *Princess Marguerite,* the "Pat" had been built in 1948 for triangle service linking Vancouver, Victoria on Vancouver Island, and Seattle, then was converted for Alaska cruising in 1963. By the time we sailed with her 15 years later, she had already spent two winters chartered to a company offering luxury warm-weather cruises from Los Angeles to Acapulco. That start-up line, Princess Cruises, had taken its name from our modest Canadian Pacific ship and never looked back.

Just after 8 AM with clouds hanging low beneath the brow of mountain peaks scattered with snow, the Princess Patricia had eased up to the wharf in Skagway and by 8:15 was fast. From the forward deck we looked down on the dock where a little train stood that in a few minutes would take us on a substantial round-trip journey into the mountains, to Lake Bennett, about 40 miles away. Dressed in olive-drab, the consist might have looked ordinary, but the majority of its cars, named for area lakes, had remarkable and deep histories. Most were parlor cars, with commodious inward-facing chairs. These included *Lake Tagish* (built by Wilmington's Harlan & Hollingsworth in 1887 for the South Pacific Coast, acquired by WP&Y in 1928 and reconfigured as a parlor car in 1937) and *Lake Dewey* (built by Jackson & Sharp, also of Wilmington, in 1889 for the Los Angeles & Redondo Railroad, acquired by WP&Y in 1901 and reconfigured as a parlor car in 1917).

Lake Lebarge, though far newer than that pair, having been built as a parlor car in 1936, was not without distinction. It was the White Pass & Yukon's first all-steel passenger car, and in 1962 it had carried Her Royal Highness, Queen Elizabeth II. Beyond that, the name probably resonates with generations of schoolchildren who read Robert W. Service's old warhorse of a poem, "The Cremation of Sam McGee." That event, welcomed by McGee, a miner tired of Alaska's frigid weather, took place "on the marge of Lake Lebarge." Rounding out our train were recently built coaches and one more car with heritage: a cupola-crowned combine built by American Car & Foundry in 1918 for the Sumpter Valley Railway and acquired by WP&Y in 1946.

For a railroad just 110.7 miles long, a branchless main line from Skagway to Whitehorse, the White Pass & Yukon Route had a rich and convoluted history—boom and bust and then boom and bust all over again. When it opened in 1900, its mission was to link the thriving gold-mining districts—Atlin, Yukon, Klondike, and White Horse, according to an early brochure—with tidewater at Skagway, located on Taiya Inlet of the Lynn Canal, at the far end of the Inland Passage, a protected waterway that extends all the way south to Vancouver and Seattle. The railroad was indeed the "Gateway to the Yukon," the slogan bannered on its wooden boxcars. Before the railroad was built, most prospectors came north by ship to Dyea, a few miles from Skagway. From there they packed supplies and headed up the rugged trail over Chilkoot Pass to Lake Lindeman.

Backed by $10 million in British capital, and under the leadership of Samuel H. Graves, who would serve as president of the railroad until 1911,

Five Alco/MLW units put their muscle into a substantial consist bound
from Skagway's Ore Dock to Whitehorse. At the tail end of the train are
a number of containers, a technology WP&Y pioneered in 1955.

construction was begun on May 27, 1898. The line was completed a little more than two years later when the last spike was driven on June 29, 1900, at Carcross (originally "caribou crossing"), Yukon Territory. Construction up into the mountains obviously presented formidable challenges, particularly on the south end of the line to White Pass Summit. Engineers blasted ledges, cuts, and tunnels and employed the bridges that would make our journey such a revelation.

The White Pass & Yukon served three political entities with both rail-borne and waterborne conveyances, so it was corporately complex. Three carriers operated as the company's railroad division: the Pacific & Arctic Railway and Navigation Company from Skagway through Alaska to White Pass; the British Columbia–Yukon Railway from White Pass through British Columbia to the Yukon border, near Pennington; and the British Yukon Railway to Whitehorse, the end of the line. The British Yukon Navigation Company and the American Yukon Navigation Company were organized in 1901 to run the company's steamboat fleet as its river division. Later, the ocean division would operate freighters between Vancouver and Skagway, and the company eventually would also have air, highway, pipeline, and petroleum divisions.

Although the boom years of the gold frenzy quickly quieted (Yukon Territory's population slipped from more than 30,000 when the railway was begun to 8,000 in 1911 and 4,000 in 1921), freight tonnages held up until World War I. Passenger volumes dropped, however, from 18,000 in the first full year of operation to 8,000 in 1916. About this time the WP&Y discovered the new gold—tourists—and began promoting recreational travel off the coastal steamships calling at Skagway. Attractive brochures touted the remote grandeur of the Yukon, often featuring lake and river steamboat connections to the rail journey. The company in 1917 built the handsome Tutshi to take passengers from Carcross to the scenic Taku Arm. Other steamers served the Yukon River from Whitehorse.

Tourism notwithstanding, the White Pass & Yukon languished: witness the fact that the railroad did not add a single locomotive to its roster from 1908, when it acquired Consolidation No. 69, to 1938, when it bought Mikado No. 70. World War II changed all that. Driven by the threat of a Japanese invasion of the West Coast, an enormous road-building project was pressed forward: the 1,523-mile Alaska–Canada Alcan Highway. Today called the Alaska Highway, it bridges countless miles of wilderness to tie Alaska to the lower 48 states. It woke up the sleepy little WP&Y, which proved to be the best available supply line to the highway. Suddenly a railroad that had operated as few as 2 trains a week was being asked to run as many as 17 a day. It was nothing short of overwhelming—so much so that, on October 1, 1942, the railroad was leased to the U.S. Army, to be run as the 770th Railway Operating Battalion. Eleven new and 17 used locomotives arrived from the

Two pairs of GE diesels meet along the shore of Summit Lake at White Pass.

south, including 7 of the Denver & Rio Grande Western's 10 outside-frame K-28 class 2-8-2's, the remaining 3 of which would become famous on Colorado's Silverton train.

When the Army lease ended in 1946, the White Pass & Yukon had a plant in many ways improved but equipment that was worn out. With the wartime highway-building boom over, there wasn't much to haul anyway, so the newly acquired locomotives were sent south for scrap. Ironically, the highway it had been so instrumental in building was a major reason for the little railway's renewed slumber. Nevertheless, the line graph of the White Pass's prosperity had a few major upswings ahead, and in the 1950s this steam-powered narrow-gauge railway began to remake itself in a remarkable way,

Modernization began in June 1954 when the first 2 of 11 shovel-nose diesels, Nos. 90 and 91, were delivered by General Electric. By then, planning was already under way for a truly monumental innovation: containerization. It seems implausible that a remote 3-foot-gauge mountain railway would be the pioneer in the intermodalism so central to mainline railroading in the twenty-first century, but that's the fact. In 1955 the world's first container ship, White Pass & Yukon's 4,000-ton *Clifford J. Rogers,* entered service, completing a ship-rail-truck link to haul 640 metal containers—8 by 8 by 7 foot boxes, tiny by today's standards—built for the service. Mining in the region was picking up, and silver-lead-zinc concentrate often filled these containers. In December 1956, dieselization continued with the arrival of three more GE's, 92–94. Another three, 95–97, came in March 1963, effectively dieselizing the railroad. All of these units were rated at 930 horsepower. The final three GE's, 98–100, delivered in May 1966, were slightly more powerful at 990 hp.

A trio of GE's dig in to roll their train out of the depot at Skagway. The wooden boxcar at the head of the consist carries the railroad's logo, "Gateway to the Yukon."

By this time the White Pass had completed a major upgrade to its inter-modal program, virtually a whole new system, actually, requiring an $8 million investment, a substantial sum at the time. In April 1965, the 6,000-ton *Frank H. Brown* had been launched for White Pass Ocean Services. Named for the White Pass president who had overseen the initial containerization, this Canadian-built vessel, a tanker as well as a container ship, was equipped with a gantry crane (from Norway) that greatly improved the loading and unloading of containers. These containers measured 8 feet by 8 feet by 25 feet 3 inches, making them more than three times the size of the original ones. Like their predecessors, they came in four versions: dry, vented, heated, and refrigerated.

Other aspects of the project included construction of a freight-handling facility in North Vancouver and improvements to the pier at Skagway; construction of freight terminals at those points, as well as at Whitehorse, where the containers were transferred to trucks; and acquisition of six "straddle carriers" to load and unload the containers from railcars and trucks. The freight-car fleet had been modernized incrementally over the previous decade, and dieselization was completed in 1964 with the retirement of 2-8-2's Nos. 72 and 73. Although it still hauled passengers in wooden coaches dating from the 1880s, the White Pass by the end of 1965 was a remarkably modern railroad.

For the next decade and a half, it would thrive, its business buoyed by increased mining activity in the Yukon. In particular, a large open-pit silver-lead-zinc mine opened in the Anvil Range feeding huge amounts of traffic to the railroad. To meet this demand, in May 1969 WP&Y acquired seven 1,200-hp hood units from Alco. By the end of the year, two of these had been destroyed in a roundhouse fire that also damaged Mikado No. 72 beyond repair. (It was sold for parts to an excursion railroad.) Replacing the lost diesels were three with identical specifications, delivered in December 1971 by Alco subsidiary (and, later, successor) Montreal Locomotive Works. In the 1970s, some of both locomotive types—the 90-Class GE shovelnoses and the 101-Class chop-nose Alco/MLW's—were given a new look, their original yellow-and-green dress (and, in the case of the GE's, "thunderbird" nose herald) replaced by white and blue, with a logo that strove to be modern.

Two of those chop-nose hood units—class engine No. 101 in original green and yellow followed by No. 110 in blue and white—led our train off the dock, past the spur to the depot and then the yards and engine house, and quickly out of town, following the Skagway River. Our expectations for the trip were vague, other than "Scenery" with a capital S. What we encountered was a route of unsurpassed scenic interest and astonishing operating challenge, with grades ranging up to 3.9 percent required to lift us from sea level to 2,885 feet at White Pass Summit, a distance of only 20 miles.

One way this climb could be calibrated was by bridges, many of them spectacular. The first was 5A, across the East Fork of the Skagway River on a horseshoe curve at timetable location "Denver," named for the Denver Glacier, which fed that branch of the river. (Bridges on the WP&Y are identified by mile number and a letter indicating their sequence within that mile. Thus 5A was the first after milepost 5, and hypothetically 5B would be the second.) The engineer slowed as we crossed Pitchfork Falls so we could appreciate the view. Then at Glacier came 14A, another curved bridge—this one over the main fork of the Skagway—again in the apex of an elevation-gaining horseshoe. From there, scaling the north wall of Glacier Gorge, we could look down and see, far below, the rails we'd just ridden.

We left the gorge by inching around a tight curve, rolling over a concrete fill bolted to sheer cliff and onto a curved wooden trestle—15C, perhaps the most picturesque single spot on the railroad. We then plunged through a wood-framed portal into Tunnel Mountain. One more notable bridge remained before the summit—18A, at an especially troublesome location. The current bridge, part of the upgrades made in 1969 to handle the Anvil business, was modestly interesting, but much less so than the original one, which was still in place: an elegant steel cantilever span with curved timber-trestle approaches that dated from 1901. It had replaced a stopgap switchback and turntable arrangement used briefly when the railroad opened.

Although it can snow heavily at White Pass, that's not where the location, and thus the railroad, got its name; rather, more than a decade before the railroad opened, this critical pass had been named for the Honorable Thomas White, Canadian minister of the interior. It's appropriate, then, that at White Pass the rails cross from the United States into Canada. We saw some of that snow and plenty more scenery on the second half of our journey to Bennett. The climb continued past Fraser, but now through a wide-open landscape of jumbled bedrock. At Fraser we had passed a water tank; fully enclosed against the cold in a square clapboard structure, it was testimony to the nature of winters in the region and a reminder that the WP&Y was then a year-round railroad. We ran along Fraser Lake and Shallow Lake and passed through Meadows. At Log Cabin station, we reached the highest point on the railroad at 2,916 feet, crossed "the Flats," then dropped down the 3.3 grade off Bennett Hill to the south end of Bennett Lake.

While our train turned on the loop at Bennett for the return journey, we had lunch at the "eating house" maintained there from the railroad's early years to feed train crews and section crews as well as passengers. We

Mikado No. 73 pops out of Tunnel Mountain
and rolls across Bridge 15C. (FACING PAGE)

inspected Mikado No. 73 and the rotary snowplow on display, with no expectation that either would be steamed again. By the time we headed back for Skagway, a warm sun had pushed through the gray, making the rugged landscape postcard-pretty. The WP&Y ran daily mixed trains in both directions, Nos. 1 and 2, and we met Whitehorse-bound No. 1, which had left Skagway two hours behind us, on our return journey. In its consist were flat cars carrying automobiles and travel trailers. The South Klondike Highway, a gravel road connecting Skagway with Carcross and the Alaska Highway at Whitehorse that had been in the works for decades, hadn't yet opened, although it would in less than two months, changing everything.

Back at Skagway, our train curved into the depot track at Skagway, dropping us there rather than on the pier. My family returned to the ship, but I had some exploring to do, beginning with the station itself. A utilitarian structure, its best feature was the mural spread across the wall above the ticket window that showed a Mikado, a steamboat, both types of diesel, a "straddle carrier," and two container ships, including the pioneering *Clifford J. Rogers*. On the counter I found a plainly printed yellow flyer called "About Your Train," intended as a caveat for those boarding No. 1. "Your train is referred to as a 'mixed daily,'" it began. "This term means both passengers and freight are carried. For this reason, we may be delayed due to switches and positioning of freight cars. We hope that any delay does not inconvenience you." The flyer continued with a statement about what made the railroad unique in 1978, calling it "the lifeline for supplies and perishable goods from 'Outside' destined for the people and businesses in this Northern Region. In addition, our trains also carry lead, copper, zinc, silver, and asbestos fiber from the Yukon Territory to the world markets."

From the depot I walked down to the yard to watch mixed No. 2, headed by a long string of containers, rumble in behind a quartet of GE shovelnoses, then hiked back to the "Pat", passing the *Klondike*, a container ship docked ahead of us. Dinner aboard in the wood-panel dining room was as wonderful as always—smoked salmon canapé, Alaska halibut with shrimp sauce, old-fashioned English plum pudding with hard sauce—with bald eagles cavorting right outside our table window. Still, I was antsy, as I wanted to photograph the "Pat" in the lovely, low, late light of those long, northerly June days. I wolfed down my pudding and left, which I could do without risk, since sailing wouldn't be until 11 PM. In addition to shots of the *Princess Patricia* and the *Klondike,* I was given a bonus: a long freight train, including lots of containers, leaving the Ore Dock behind four Alco/MLW units, Whitehorse-bound.

As it turned out, this would be my last glimpse of the WP&Y as a freight hauler. When I returned a quarter-century later, in 2003, this time in early June for a weekend of special trains for photographers, the railroad had been

GE shovel-nose diesels and Mikado No. 73 pose together
in morning sunlight at Glacier, Alaska.

hugely transformed, thriving as never before, but only after a near-death experience. When the railway's major customer, Cyprus Anvil, closed its mine
and concentrator in June 1982, the WP&Y seemed doomed. It shut down in
October—and slept until 1988. By then, the cruise trade to Alaska had begun to boom, so the railroad reopened as far as Bennett solely as a passenger
hauler. For the 1988 season, the WP&Y carried 37,000 passengers, a number
that had swollen by more than tenfold when I made my 2003 visit. While the
Princess Patricia had brought about 200 of us, a full ship, to Skagway and was
one of but a handful of vessels then in the Alaska cruise trade, twenty-first-
century cruise ships routinely carry 2,500 and more. In 2003 I saw as many
as five ships in Skagway at once.

I also saw No. 73 in steam, the diesels back in their handsome green-
and-yellow dress, and trains full of ship passengers leaving Skagway in the
morning on trolley car headways. I saw the railroad reopened along the shore
of Lake Bennett north to Carcross.

The concluding sentence of the yellow flyer from 1978 said this: "We hope
that combining the historical aspects of your trip with the commerce of today
will be a memorable and unique adventure"—a wish every bit as valid in 2003,
though the commerce was as different as night and day.

In a view from the *morro grande* itself—the "large, rounded hill"—a 2-10-2 pounds upgrade. (ABOVE)

The crew of 2-10-4 No. 313 is ready to head east out of Pino Yard. (LEFT)

3

MAGIC AT MORRO GRANDE

MORRO GRANDE. NOW THAT'S A NAME TO SAVOR. WHEN I looked at a map of Brazil's meter-gauge Teresa Cristina Railway, it jumped off the page, sorting itself out from the other place-names: Tubarão, Pineirinho, Içara, Jaguaruna, Capivari, Imbituba. For one thing, it had a reassuringly familiar look and sound to it—no perplexing diacritics or Portuguese inflections, odd to the ear of English speakers. For another, it had ready-made narrow-gauge resonances, thanks to the Denver & Rio Grande.

But when Laurel and I visited in March 1984, Morro Grande had more than just its handle to recommend it. The little village straddling the tracks of the Teresa Cristina, though unexceptional in social or economic terms, was special in railroading. Not that there was much rail plant—just a passing track, a square, yellowish stucco station with wide eaves, and a concrete barrel of a water tank completely lacking in aesthetic appeal. But that was enough.

The gritty, coal-smoky magic of Morro Grande was really a distillation of the wonder of the entire Teresa Cristina Railway: the Estrada de Ferro Doña Teresa Cristina, a roughly 100-mile-long (including branches), ex-

It's a busy day at Pineirinho Yard, where coal hoppers are gathered to
be forwarded on to Tubarão and then to the port at Imbituba.

clusively coal-hauling, mostly steam-powered, no-nonsense railroad in an
unremarkable part of southern Brazil. There was nothing effete about this
line except its name, which honors the wife of Dom Pedro II, Brazil's last
emperor, whose reign was peaceful and prosperous. What raised the Teresa Cristina from the obscurity in which it once labored and brought it to
the general notice of steam enthusiasts in the United States was its locomotive roster. For years, the stalwarts of the railroad were handsome 174-ton
Alco and Baldwin 300-class 2-10-4s's, which numbered 13 when I went calling, with one lost earlier in a wreck. This army of Texas types was hale and
hearty then, but not long afterwards they were decimated by a pernicious
plague of firebox cracks and all removed from service, replaced by a fleet of
General Electric diesels. I had been, in fact, just in time.

Testimony to the then-booming coal business, and all the more significant in light of the subsequent failure of the 2-10-4's, had been the 1978 ac-

quisition of 12 2-10-2's from Argentina, most of them built in Czechoslovakia by Skoda in 1949 for Argentina's Ferrocarril Nacional General Belgrano. Just two had been built in 1937 in Germany by Henschel, after a Baldwin proto-type from 1921, which explains the class's American appearance. Eventually all 12 would be overhauled, converted from oil-burning to coal, and placed in service on the Teresa Cristina as Nos. 400–411.

The 2-10-2's had attracted attention and photographers before going to Brazil, for among their assignments on the Belgrano had been tackling the fa-mous Ramal C-14 line to Chile, with its switchbacks, spiral loops, and 14,680-foot-elevation crossing of the Andes at Chorrillos Pass. The Santa Fe types faced no similar challenges in their new home in Brazil. There they were just role players in a workaday routine that had become for American enthusiasts one of the most charismatic and nostalgic steam shows in the world.

Here is the stage on which that show played. Dating from 1884, an even century before I found it, the Teresa Cristina ran across southern Brazil from the seaport of Imbituba for 76 miles to the most distant mine at Rio Fiorita. The heart of the railroad was the small city of Tubarão, roughly halfway be-tween Imbituba and Pineirinho Yard, which is on the outskirts of the city of Criciúma. "Pino" Yard was the marshalling point for loaded hoppers coming in from three mine branches that radiated from it, including the one to Rio Fiorita. Although slim-gauge, largely steam-powered, and short, the Teresa Cristina was unmistakably big-time. In fact, it boasted the highest tonnage-per-mile figure of any component of the national system, the Rede Ferroviar-ia Federal S.A. (RFFSA), of which it had become a part in 1957. It was the system's 12th Division, and the only one disconnected from the others.

The Teresa Cristina had been built by British interests, taken over by the Brazilian government in 1902, returned to private ownership in 1918, and tak-en back by the government in 1940. In 1983, a record 7.2 millions tons of coal had been hauled in the railroad's 868 wooden-bodied, bottom-discharge hop-per cars, assembled into an average of 38 trains a day. Trains typically were 24 cars long, handled by a single locomotive. All passing tracks accommodated 60-car trains, allowing doubleheading, an only occasional practice.

The paving of a highway that paralleled the railway had killed all trains but coal drags, so I could experience the Teresa Cristina only as a spectator, not as a rider. But at the time of my visit, coal trains ran around the clock, shutting down only on Sundays. On that day, when nothing much would move, the locomotive fleet steamed softly on the ready tracks at the Tubarão shops. In addition to the 10-coupled engines, there were six Mikados that covered the switching at Capivari and Tubarão: Nos. 153 through 157 (Alco 1941) and 160 (Baldwin 1945). Labeled "Oficinas" on rail maps, the shop complex—which included a machine shop, foundry, boiler shop, pattern shop, and locomotive service area—was in downtown Tubarão.

My visit to the Teresa Cristina had gotten off to a rocky start. We'd flown to Rio de Janeiro and then south to Florianopolis, where we rented a Volkswagen Beetle for a hellish high-speed drive at dusk, pushed along by racing trucks, sharing the road with horse carts and pedestrians, heading further south to Laguna, a seacoast town not far from Tubarão. There we were booked at a rather spiffy beach resort that was virtually empty, since it was out of season. As we turned our car over to the doorman for parking, we noticed that the compound was gated and surrounded by a high (if handsome) fence.

Up early the next morning to get in a full day of train-watching, we called for our VW. As it inched into view from the parking lot, I saw with sinking heart that the windshield was completely broken out, and the front seats were littered with crazed safety glass. The improbable explanation for this centered on the region's alleged extreme variation in barometric pressure, a theory that we weren't ready to buy. With less than three full days available to explore the Teresa Cristina, I panicked as precious minutes slipped away. But one of the hotel staff drove the car to a repair shop with me, and in less than an hour I was on my way to Tubarão.

Once there, I did as I'd been advised and headed for the railroad's downtown offices on Rui Barbosa. At the front desk, I asked for Dr. Gilberto Cabral, *Chefe da Divisão:* the man in charge. Genial and helpful and a fluent English speaker, Cabral seemed every bit the steam fan he was reputed to be. In fact, many observers gave Cabral much of the credit for keeping the railroad in steam. From him I received not only the authorization I'd sought for visiting the shops and for lineside photography but also an invitation. Would Laurel and I like to join Gilberto and Yara, his wife, for dinner at their house? *Enginero* Oldemar Michel, the railroad's chief of operations, whom I'd also met in the division offices, would join us, along with his wife, Icléa.

Following the directions he had given me, we drove our freshly glazed VW up to an attractive single-level brick house. It struck us as solidly upper middle class in what was evidently a good neighborhood of Tubarão. Yara greeted us at the front door, then led us to an enclosed patio behind the house, where Gilberto was grilling a variety of meats—beef, sausages, chicken, a traditional Brazilian *churrasco*. We dined comfortably and informally with the Cabrals, their young children, and the Michels. After dinner Yara was eager to show us some precious things, vases and other artifacts, that she and Gilberto had collected in their travels. They were in the formal living room. For us to enter, she had to unlock the wrought-iron gate securing the room.

Eventually it was time to leave. We said our good-byes, then walked to our car in the cool of evening. It was at that point that we noticed the uniformed guard marching back and forth in front of the house, toting an automatic rifle.

Mikado No. 160, built by Baldwin in 1945, switches
coal hoppers at Tubarão's Henri Lage Yard.

Back to railroading. From the shop at Oficinas, every hour or two a Texas
or Santa Fe would chuff off through the town to the Henri Lage yard, where
it coupled onto a string of empties assembled by Mikado 160. The big engine
would then head southwest through Jaguaruna, Morro Grande, Esplanada,
and Içara—sites of the four passing tracks on this section of the Teresa Cristina—and on to Pino Yard. Generally, there were also two or three trains
a day that left the main line at Esplanada to serve the 15-mile Urussanga
Branch. From Pinheirinho, three 300's or 400's assigned to mine-run duty
scattered the empties at tipples along three branches and collected loads,
bringing them to the yard. Once the loads were assembled into a train, a 2-10-
2 or 2-10-4 would tie on for the run back to Tubarão or, more frequently, to
the huge coal-washing plant and electric generating station at Capivari, just
3 miles beyond.

Diesels first dented the steam monopoly on the Teresa Cristina in October 1981, when three 1,200-horsepower B-B G12's—built in Brazil by General

In Tubarão, the Oficinas engine terminal is full of locomotives, many live, some under repair. This facility
included a machine shop, foundry, and pattern shop,
along with a servicing area.

Motors in 1958–59 for the Porto Alegre Railway, about 150 miles down the
coast of Brazil from Tubarão—were brought over and for a time became
the regular power on trains on the scenic line from Capivari to the docks at
Imbituba. One G12 could pull only as much as a 2-10-2 or 2-10-4, but the diesels' ability to M.U. gave them an edge. Although steam sometimes would be
pressed into service when a ship was in port and the volume of loads became
more than the three units could handle, during my visit internal combustion
ruled the 29-mile segment of line between washer and port.

Everything else was handled by steam. The 2-10-2's and 2-10-4's, near
equals in heft and hauling power, were dispatched interchangeably on both
road jobs and mine runs. Two of the 2-10-4's had been built by Alco for the
Teresa Cristina in 1940, while the balance of the fleet were Baldwins built
that same year (except for No. 311, which was seven years younger) and purchased secondhand from the Central of Brazil and Noroeste. The Texas types
were rated at 41,000 pounds tractive force, while the Belpaire-boilered ex-
Argentine Santa Fes, though with smaller fireboxes, were slightly more pow-

erful, with a tractive force of 44,800 pounds. Aside from the European-style wye-braced smokebox hinges with which most had been refit, the 2-10-4's were hauntingly reminiscent of North American steam; some saw echoes of Louisville & Nashville Berkshires in their graceful lines. After being around them for a few days, I easily lost a sense of their diminutiveness, and when an engineer would appear in the gangway, providing irrefutable evidence of scale, I was startled. The locomotives all looked to be well maintained, but they wore the road grime that was their accreditation as workaday haulers and burners of coal.

Smack in the middle of the then-all-steam trunk line was Morro Grande. All trains to and from the mines passed through there, and they lingered. Locomotives in either direction invariably stopped for water at the squat concrete tank. In a way, Morro Grande was a Brazilian version of Thurmond, West Virginia, on the Chesapeake & Ohio. Although Morro Grande does not lie in a steep valley, as does Thurmond, in both towns storefronts and houses faced the tracks up close, as if in recognition that the most notable local events took place on the railroad.

When I showed up at Morro Grande on my first day to see the Teresa Cristina's locomotives, I knew right away that I had found a special place. I did explore the railroad's other dimensions—Pino Yard and the mine branches; Oficinas, where a half-dozen 300's and 400's stood disassembled in various stages of restoration; and Capivari, where a chunky little Baldwin Mike, class of 1941, was assigned, along with a Texas-type, to switch the washing plant and generating station. But during the next three days, I kept returning to Morro Grande and the coal drags that shuttled by. I liked the tile-roofed houses of crumbling stucco that lined the town's main street (and the railroad) with their pale pastels, and the *lanchonette*—deep and dark inside, cool-looking, open at the front, indiscriminately dispensing snacks and sodas, beer, and Brazilian whiskey. A train crew, having watered their engine and now waiting for a meet with mine-bound empties, parked at the *lanchonette's* doorstep and watered themselves.

I liked the ox and donkey carts that rounded out the town's transportation picture, and the dogs that skulked under the water tower and around the depot, running in and out among the hopper cars at rest while locomotives took water. I liked the brickworks in the area, examples of an industry that seemed properly marginal, human, and earthy for this place of steam-powered coal trains. I liked the *morro grande* itself, the large, rounded hill that bumped up just southwest of town. Its far slope provided an admirable, unobstructed vantage for watching a Texas or Santa Fe roaring out of Esplanada with 30 loaded hoppers, making a run at the grade ahead, exhaust staccato as the train rushed down a long tangent, then veered off on a graceful curve to avoid collision with the hill. Before long, the locomotive was down on its hands and

With the depot in the background, a 2-10-2
takes water at Morro Grande.

knees, climbing steeply while slicing the hill in a sharp cut, stack talk now
sharp, labored, and loud as it echoed in close quarters.

I liked the depot—heavy, no-frills, totally lacking in distinctive archi-
tectural fillips but good to look at nonetheless for its classic shape and as a
reminder that the coal hauler had indeed operated passenger trains, albeit
two decades earlier. And I particularly liked the young Brazilian who worked
there and tried to hurdle the language barrier to tell me what train movements
were coming up. The traditional "what, where, when, why" litany of the in-
quisitive train watcher was futile. He spoke no English and I no Portuguese.
(I had an ultimately useless Portuguese phrase book that posed elaborate and
stilted questions, the answers to which I couldn't possibly have understood,
but nothing like "Has the train left Içara yet?") But with gyrations, gesticulations, impromptu maps, and locomotives numbers scribbled on scraps of
paper, there *was* communication—and goodwill, too, readily conveyed by
smiles, waves, and the peculiarly affirmative thumbs-up gesture that is a regular part of Brazilian body language.

On one occasion I could tell from a certain agitation in his manner that something out of the ordinary was in the offing. He grabbed a pad of official forms, tore off a sheet, flipped it over, and carefully inscribed two numbers—405 and 311—then gestured toward Tubarão. Two trains coming on close headway, I assumed. But what appeared was even better: a doubleheader, the only one I would see. From what I had gathered from talking with Gilberto Cabral, it was a relative rarity.

While the two locomotives were stopped in Morro Grande taking water, a whistle sounded to the west, announcing the arrival of 403 with a string of loaded hoppers. The Santa Fe clanked through town on the passing track, eased by the depot, and came to a halt with a sigh of air. Since the water tank only served the main line, the 403 would have to wait until the double-shotted little giants left town with their empties, then back out onto the main and pull forward to the tank for its refreshment. As that departure neared, the firemen stoked their charges in earnest, blocking out the sun and thus settling a premature dusk over Morro Grande. The engineers finished oiling around, a ritual not confined by national borders. Suddenly, the shriek of 405's European-style whistle pierced the heavy air, laden with pungent coal smoke and alive with the roar of steam rushing through lifted pop valves.

Again the banshee wailed, and the doubleheader was moving, stomping out of town and kicking up a real ruckus. The offbeat cadence of the two 10-coupled locomotives literally shook the earth as the hoggers hauled out hard on their throttles and the hoppers began to rock and roll and rattle. No. 405 hooted for the grade crossing at the end of town, and 311's chime whistle sang in counterpoint as the doubleheader brawled its way west under twin towers of smoke.

In comparison, Capivari-bound 403's switching, watering, and departure were positively stately. Not until both trains were well out of earshot, and Morro Grande had settled back into the depths of a rural afternoon stillness broken only by the cries of children playing and the barking of dogs, did the sun burn through the coal smoke.

Riding the Talyllyn Railway, this is the view of the Welsh countryside from the footplate of No. 1 running upgrade toward Nant Gwernol. (ABOVE)

No. 1, *Talyllyn*, pauses at Nant Gwernol, the end of the line. In a few moments it will run around its train and head back to Tywyn Wharf Station. (BELOW)

4

WALES · REALLY NARROW

I N CENTRAL WALES, A BEAUTIFUL LAND OF LUSH VALLEYS and rugged, rock-ribbed seacoast, old ways lingered on. The scale of buildings and machinery remained intimate and human. Once the economy of Wales had been based largely on what could be carved from the earth, primarily coal in the south and slate further north. When I visited in August 1987, however, the Welsh economy was based instead on mining the wallets of the many tourists drawn there by the region's remarkable scenery and fascinating antiquities, among them a handful of narrow-gauge steam railways widely promoted as the "Great Little Trains of Wales."

Among these lines, the Talyllyn Railway owns a very particular distinction that raises it above its fellows. It was the first railway in Britain, and perhaps the first anywhere, saved from abandonment and kept in operation by volunteers. Thus it has two histories: first as a gritty slate-hauler and player in the Industrial Revolution and second as a pioneering preserved line, a model for many that would follow in Britain, America, and elsewhere. As a preserved railroad, it has its own impressive history.

The Talyllyn Railway was created by an act of Parliament in 1865 to haul split and trimmed slate down the mountain from a quarry that had been

established 18 years earlier at Bryn Eglwys (Welsh for "church on the hill")
in the valley of the Nant Gwernol. The line would terminate on the Cardigan
Bay coast at Tywyn, where the slate could be interchanged with the standard-
gauge Aberystwyth & Welsh Coast Railway, which over the years became the
Cambrian Railways, then the Great Western, then—when I visited—British
Rail's Cambrian Coast Line. All this time the Talyllyn Railway was the Talyl-
lyn Railway, built in 2-foot 3-inch gauge—the same as the nearby Corris,
Machynlleth & River Dovey, constructed in 1859 as a horse tramway to haul
slate from a quarry on the opposite side of the mountain from Bryn Eglwys.
Steam traction came to the Corris Railway 20 years later.

The Talyllyn, on the other hand, would be steam-hauled from the
beginning. To that end, locomotive No. 1, *Talyllyn*, was delivered in September 1865 as a 0-4-0 saddle tanker and helped in the final stages of construction
of the line. The next year No. 2, another 0-4-0T, arrived on the property. Both
were products of Fletcher, Jennings & Co. These two were the only locomotives owned by the TR before the preservation era, and both were there when
I visited more than 120 years after their arrival.

In fact, when I was invited to ride the footplate (we Americans would call
it a "cab ride") on the TR in August 1987, it turned out that the locomotive
I drew was the progenitor himself, *Talyllyn*, and still spry. It had long been a
0-4-2T, a trailing truck having been added in 1867 (at age 2) to correct "exces-
sive vertical oscillation" on the footplate, caused by too much overhang at the
rear. This I took to mean that the cab bucked up and down in a disconcerting
way.

As I surveyed this diminutive antique before trying to board, I wondered
how I could possibly squeeze into this tiny cab with the driver and fireman
and still give the latter room to wield a "scoop," locomotive-cab argot for
shovel. (And speaking of argot, as an American visitor, I found one of the
charms of British trains to be the frequent skewing of railway terminology
from stateside usage. An engineer, for instance, is a driver, who works on the
footplate, not in the cab. A conductor is a guard, who works in a carriage,
not in a coach, though a group of carriages does comprise "coaching stock."
Freight trains are "goods workings," made up of wagons, not cars.)

The quality of Lilliputian diminution was no doubt a part of the Talyllyn Railway's charm. All five of the line's operable steam locomotives, the
newest of which dated from 1921 (though all had been extensively rebuilt),
were little jewels: gleaming green paint trimmed in black and red, and impeccably polished brass. No. 1, measuring just 18 feet end to end, was actually
the longest of the fleet. This American's eye, used to full-sized railroading,
was bemused by the driver's seemingly hulking size filling the locomotive's
cramped gangway and by the fact that a lineside observer had to hunker down
to study valve gear and driving wheels.

At least as important as smallness in explaining the fascination of the Talyllyn, however, is its heritage as a no-nonsense enterprise. It was a serious business, toting countless tons of slate down the mountain over a right-of-way still intact, behind locomotives still in steam. Right from the beginning provisions were made for passengers; the four carriages delivered in 1866 and 1867 to haul farmers to town, quarrymen to work, and children to school remained as fully loaded as ever in 1987, still rattling through the lush Welsh countryside, but filled with tourists and railway enthusiasts.

I was to ride the 12:50 PM train from Tywyn Wharf Station to the end of the line at Nant Gwernol, 7.25 miles distant. (*Nant* is the Welsh word for "river.") Though Tywyn is a coastal town, "wharf" has nothing to do with boats or ships but refers to the loading dock over which slate was transferred from the TR's little wagons to standard-gauge cars. Some rusted narrow-gauge rails remained along it, as did the tiny turntable—just long enough to turn a single slate wagon 90 degrees and head it down the wharf for transloading.

As departure time neared, General Manager D. Woodhouse (in Britain, railway officials seemed even more disinclined than in the United States to acknowledge owning first names) took me to the crew room in the back of the Wharf station, a venerable building housing the booking office. Its construction of brick, rather than the otherwise ubiquitous slate, suggested to me that it predated the line's completion, which would have opened easy access to cheap slate from the quarry. There I shook hands with Winston McKenna, the loquacious fireman with whom I'd be riding, and John MacDougal, the more taciturn driver.

"You're at the birthplace of railway preservation," McKenna said as we walked out to board the locomotive. "And a bit of luck: today we've got No. 1. Back in 1865, it was shipped by sea to Aberdovey, just down the coast." He pointed to a short, four-wheeled coach in red livery, trimmed out in wood, the second car from the locomotive. "No. 2 here is one of the original four carriages," he said. An ornate plaque on its frame read "Brown Marshall & Co. Builder, Birmingham." The car was then more than 120 years old, as was the steam engine.

Directly behind the locomotive was another carriage of note: No. 17, a bogie coach (that is, one with trucks versus a smaller two-axle car) built in 1898 by Metropolitan Carriage and Wagon Co. Ltd. for the neighboring Corris Railway, on which it ran until 1930, when passenger service was suspended. All operations ceased in 1947. The bones of the Corris—which shared the unusual gauge of 2 feet 3 inches with the Talyllyn and just two other railways in Britain, the long-defunct Campbeltown & Machrihanish on the Mull of Kintyre in Scotland and Plynlimon & Hafan Tramway in Wales—would provide good picking for the preserved TR. Some Corris rails and ties came over from a scrap dealer, locomotives 3 and 4 (both of which were in steam during my visit) were purchased at modest cost in 1951, an 1885 brake van was acquired privately and donated to TR, and No. 17 arrived on the Talyllyn after a stint as a greenhouse and garden shed on a local farm. This handsome coach entered service in 1960, again wearing the rich brown Corris livery.

Behind these two historic carriages were four built in the preservation years: one four-wheel open-sided car and three bogie coaches with body style reminiscent of the original stock. TR's roster of two cars for the guard (that also carry luggage and packages) and 21 passenger carriages also included a pair of four-wheel cars that originally ran on the Glyn Valley Tramway.

A curious twist is that all TR coaching stock is one-sided, opening only to the north, the side of the tracks on which all platforms were built. This anomaly dates from the railway's opening, when Captain H. W. Tyler came to inspect the line for the Board of Trade and give its necessary blessing. He found a lack of clearance for trains passing between bridge abutments—1 foot 11 inches rather than 2 feet 6 inches. The pragmatic, homespun solution: permanently secure all doors on the "off" side. Remove the hardware, and bar the drop windows so passengers couldn't lean out. This allowed the tracks under the bridges to be slightly skewed to the south, providing proper clearance for the north, opening side of the train.

I stepped up onto the footplate of No. 1 and stationed myself just behind the firebox. Since *Talyllyn* was set up for right-side driving, not the norm in Britain, MacDougal was at my right elbow; at my left was Fireman McKenna. MacDougal eased out the "regulator"—the throttle—and we were on our way, squeezing through one of those tight underpasses, then rolling through a "cutting" and on into Pendre Yard and station, the primary Tywyn stop in the pre-preservation years. Pendre had always been and remained TR's maintenance headquarters. The North and West Carriage Sheds have been built since preservation, but the engine shed and well-equipped workshop are weathered slate buildings that date from the era of the line's opening. Inside was locomotive No. 2, *Dolgoch,* the stalwart that kept the railway running through the last years before preservation.

We rolled past the shops and eased to a stop at the station.

"Are you traveling?" McKenna asked a potential passenger on the platform—looking him directly in the eye, so small is *Talyllyn*. The fireman's tone was conversational, no shouting needed, since these little locomotives are remarkably gentle creatures, soft-spoken. The chuff of exhaust, the hiss of steam, the muffled roar of the firebox: all are muted statements compared with the cacophony typical of a standard-gauge steam-locomotive cab.

The Pendre blockman handed McKenna a "token"—a key-shaped device some 6 inches long—that gave us the right to proceed on to Brynglas, the first passing "loop." (In Britain, trains cross, rather than meet, on loops, not passing sidings.) Then, leaning out of the gangway, McKenna spotted the go-ahead wave from the guard.

"Right away it is," he called across to the driver, who then hauled on the whistle cord and eased open the throttle. With that shrill warning we snuffled off, across the railway's only gated level crossing and out into the countryside. The rails would climb virtually all the way to Nant Gwernol, but always on a moderate gradient. Amid farmlands we rolled by short platforms at Fach Goch and Cynfal Bridge, demand stops only, before pausing at an old slate shelter deep in the shade of trees at Rhydyronen. The oldest intermediate station on the line, it dates from 1867.

No. 1's cab and controls were a marvel of simplicity. Atop the backhead were a steam gauge and a pair of safety valves, all highly polished brass, and below them a water glass and a ratcheted regulator handle thrusting toward the driver. With a miniature scoop—truly toylike, no more than 3 feet in length, handle and all—McKenna dug into the bunker right in front of him, then tossed big chunks of coal through the firebox door at my feet. With a small broom, he brushed coal dust off the footplate. The entire space was spotless: scrubbed, wiped, polished, swept.

Both *Talyllyn* and *Dolgoch* were delivered with open footplates, no shelter at all for the crew. Almost immediately rudimentary cabs had been fitted: basically just metal sheets that curved over the top and wrapped around the back. Brass-rimmed portholes—"spectacle glasses"—on both the driver's side and the fireman's side provided visibility, although I found it just as easy to poke my head out the wall-less side of the cab.

At Brynglas we crossed a "down" train with locomotive No. 3 in charge. In all 85 years of pre-preservation operation, the TP ran on a "one engine in steam" basis, and therefore without passing loops, signaling, tokens, or any of the trappings of multiple-train operations. In the years since the line's acquisition by the Talyllyn Railway Preservation Society, the loop at Brynglas, as well as one further up the line at Quarry Siding—have been built. When I rode, the "high summer" schedule called for four locomotives in steam, with three trains on the line.

No. 3, now named *Sir Haydn,* was one of the pair of Corris Railway locomotives that had been stalwart performers for the preserved TR. The Talyllyn debut of No. 3 was inauspicious, however, perhaps the most remarkable contretemps described by L. T. C. Rolt in his highly readable *Railway Adventure.* (Rolt, the man most responsible for saving the Talyllyn and forming the preservation society, served as the line's general manager for its first two years in preservation, the period covered in his book.) No. 3, one of a trio of 0-4-0 saddle tankers built in 1878 for Corris by Hughes Locomotive & Tramway Engine Co. at its Falcon Works in Loughborough, became an 0-4-2T in 1900. When it was bought by the TRPS and pressed into service, an unhappy combination of its narrow wheel treads and TR's over-gauge track, the result of decades of deferred maintenance, led to its embarrassing penchant for falling between the rails. Problems with both track and wheels were quickly addressed, and Sir Haydn has given good service ever since—ditto the much more modern No. 4, the other ex-Corris Locomotive, an 0-4-0T built by Kerr Stuart in 1921 and named *Edward Thomas* on the TR.

Back in 1911, Henry Haydn Jones, a local politician and businessman, bought the Bryn Eglwys Quarry and the TR from W. H. McConnel, son of the railway's first chairman. By then the McConnels had sucked whatever good there was out of the operations, and for the next four decades Jones (who became a member of Parliament and was knighted as Sir Haydn in 1937 in part because of his work with the Talyllyn) kept the modest little railway running more or less as a labor of love and public benefaction. Right from the beginning he gave Edward Thomas, who had been with TR since 1897, the daily responsibility of running the railroad. Thomas remained general manager right up to preservation and then stayed around to help the Society get on its feet. Sir Haydn vowed that the Talyllyn would not be shut down while he lived, and he was good to his word. His death in 1950, at age 87, ushered in the preservation era, the early part of which saw the naming of the Corris locomotives *Sir Haydn* and *Edward Thomas* to memorialize the two men who kept the line limping along for nearly 40 years.

From the footplate of No. 1, I watched as the narrow rails ahead crawled out on the hillside ledge they would occupy for much of the remainder of the trip.

"Best example of a glacial valley in northern Europe," McKenna said as the landscape opened up. Cader Idris, the region's dominant peak, loomed ahead. We chuffed into Dolgoch Woods—"very slippery in poor weather," according to McKenna—then through a cutting, across a three-arch viaduct spanning the rushing Nant Dolgoch, and into Dolgoch station, where we stopped to take water and unload the numerous passengers ready for a scenic walk to Dolgoch Falls or headed for the Dolgoch Hotel.

We whistled off and before long came to the passing loop at Quarry Siding, empty this trip. The blockman's green flag showed clearly against the white "siding board," so MacDougal notched out the regulator and we continued on. Blockman and fireman exchanged tokens on the move.

"Quarry Siding–Abergynolwyn," McKenna read aloud from the token before placing it in a rack on the cab side. Abergynolwyn had been the upper terminus for passengers for 11 decades, until 1976, when the final three-quarters of a mile of track to Nant Gwernol, previously restricted to goods and mineral trains, was opened to excursionists. At Abergynolwyn we met a down train with No. 6, *Douglas,* in charge. (Built in 1918 by Andrew Barclay Sons & Co. Ltd. for the Royal Air Force Construction Corps, this originally 2-foot-gauge 0-4-0T has low drivers and can be hard on the track.) Beyond the station this former mineral line swung through a series of reverse curves and into the narrowing, rock-faced ravine of the Nant Gwernol. Through the trees, far below in the valley, I saw the village of Abergynolwyn, built to house the workers of the Bryn Eglwys Quarry.

"Look, there," McKenna said, gesturing toward a derelict wooden drum at trackside, the last remains of the winding house that had once controlled an inclined railway down which cars loaded with coal and supplies for the townspeople of Abergynolwyn were lowered. "They say that the sidings ran right up to the back doors of the houses, where the coal was unloaded."

Tracks end at Nant Gwernol at the foot of the incline that brought slate down from the quarry. All the inclines were two-track and "self-acting," using the weight of the loaded wagons going down to raise the empties up the sloped planes. Bryn Eglwys, once a substantial operation employing 300 men and producing 300,000 tons of roofing slate and slabs, finally closed in 1947 because of the declining demand for slate. For decades before that it had been a struggling operation at best, as frail an enterprise as the little railway that served it.

At Nant Gwernol, *Talyllyn* ran around its train, then hauled it back to Abergynolwyn for a refreshment stop. While we waited for time, McKenna and McDougal took me for a tour of the handsome wooden signal cabin (stateside we'd call it an operating tower) and introduced me to Janet Cox, the "block lady" who worked there. She and her husband, John, the Abergynolwyn station master, were among the army of volunteers that made possible the Talyllyn's survival. In fact, virtually all the work on the TR was done by volunteers, serving as drivers, firemen, guards, and booking clerks. About 95 percent of the engine crews were volunteers, including both McKenna and MacDougall, although the latter had been a paid shopman at Pendre for seven years. In addition, work parties formed on weekends year-round performed track work and built, painted, and maintained the coaching stock. The Preservation Society, founded in 1950 during a meeting at the Hotel Imperial in Birmingham, had done its job well.

The low point for the Talyllyn railway had come in 1945, when the line was closed for a year while *Dolgoch* was rebuilt. *Talyllyn,* which Rolt called "a forlorn and rusty of object" in *Railway Adventure,* was expected never to run again. The railway did open in the summer of 1946, but winter running, which had been only twice weekly at the last, was gone for good. However,

In this view from the signal cabin at Abergynolwyn, Janet Cox hands a token to the driver of No. 4, the *Edward Thomas,* giving him permission to travel on to Nant Gwernol. (ABOVE)

The Electric Key Token machine at Abergynolwyn. (LEFT)

from then on summer workings became secure, eventually showing dramatic growth. In 1951, the first season under Preservation Society auspices, a record 15,000 passengers rode. That jumped to 22,000 in 1952, and by 1959 the count had swelled to 70,000.

From the first year in preservation, full of surprises and crises, the former blue-collar slate hauler began to assume a middle-class stability, with a right of way far better than ever before, new buildings, new signaling and train control, and an impressive roster of old and new locomotives and carriages, all gleaming in fresh paint lovingly applied. But everything has a price, as Rolt eloquently suggested in *Railway Adventure:* "Despite our pride in what has been achieved, some of us cannot help feel a twinge of nostalgic regret as we recall the pioneering days when train service was maintained by guess and by God over a way that was far from permanent," he wrote, perfectly pinpointing the ironic cost typical of preservation. "Yet such a condition of romantic decrepitude could not be perpetuated. The choice was between death and a new life and although the Talyllyn railway of today has a new look, the old spirit lives on as strongly as ever."

At Abergynolwyn, Janet Cox showed me around the signal cabin: the throws, the track diagram, and the EKT—"Electric Key Token"—that controls train movements on the line. These machines along the line are electrically interlocked, and a second token granting permission for operation over a particular stretch of track cannot be released until the first one is returned to a machine at some location. We heard No. 4, *Edward Thomas*, whistling at the far end of the passing loop with the "up" train. It came and went, leaving us to be on our way back to Tywyn, back to interchange with British Rail's Cambrian Coast Line "Sprinter" M.U. trains, back to the real world of 1988, where railways were standard-gauge, diesel-powered, and impersonal.

Celtic Circle

A circle, however angular and misshapen, is the geometric form most endearing to the traveler, especially to someone riding the rails just for fun. In 1986 I'd been able to plot just such an excursion, a trip for its own sake, starting and ending in Shrewsbury, far west in England's middle section, near the Welsh border. In fact, northern Wales offered a circle close to perfect—not in symmetry but certainly in scenery—that included, on British Rail, the Cambrian Coast Line's long flirtation with Cardigan Bay, the mountain-girt Conwy Valley Line, and the North Wales Coast Line. The best segment of all, however, wasn't standard-gauge but the 2-foot-gauge (more or less) Ffestiniog. To be able to use a historic, narrow-gauge, steam-powered train as a link in a through routing was a unique pleasure.

I left Shrewsbury aboard a brand-new British Rail "Sprinter," an M.U. diesel train that, to tell the truth, was quiet, utilitarian, and not ideally suited for sightseeing. Our first stop was at a Victorian brick station where the sign read "Trallwng/Welshpool," a bilingual tip-off that we'd entered Wales. Had I disembarked and walked a few blocks through town I could have found the steam-powered, narrow-gauge Welshpool & Llanfair Light Railway, one of the "Great Little Trains of Wales." Eight miles long, it was opened in 1903 primarily to haul farmers and their produce through a lush countryside that remains pastoral today. Later we paused at Machynlleth, where half our train split off and, at Dovey Junction, headed south to the seacoast city of Aberystwyth. Had I been aboard those cars, I could have made an across-the-platform transfer at Aberystwyth to British Rail's own steam-powered narrow-gauge railway, the Vale of Rheidol, for a grueling and scenic climb to Devil's Bridge.

However, I'd chosen the Pwllheli-bound section, which would offer fine views of Cardigan Bay. We passed Tywyn, where I might have disembarked for the Talyllyn, but didn't,

Blanche (left) and sister *Linda* at the Ffestiniog Railway's Harbour Station at Porthmadog.

and later Fairbourne, the terminus for the narrowest of the Welsh narrow gauges, the 12½-inch-gauge Fairbourne Railway. Again I stayed aboard, but at Minffordd I did disembark, and walked through an underpass and up some stairs to the Ffestiniog Railway's white-trimmed stone station. The 1-foot 11½ inch-gauge rails seemed delicate ribbons compared to the standard-gauge world I'd just left. Appearances can be deceiving, however, and in its way the Ffestiniog was a big-time railroad, with 11 weekday round-trips. "It's a bloody commuter operation," according to Talyllyn fireman Winston McKenna.

Within minutes of my arrival in Minffordd (for this was a carefully and tightly timed connection), a distant, shrill whistle sounded, announcing the train's arrival from the Harbour Station at Porthmadog, the railway's headquarters, about 2 miles away. A green locomotive, diminutive but powerful and tricked out in brass, appeared at the head of eight dark-red coaches. The steamer was *Linda*, built for the Penrhyn Quarry Railway in 1893 by the Hunslet Engine Company of Leeds and acquired by the Ffestiniog, along with twin *Blanche*, in 1963.

The guard unlocked a compartment for me, then collected my fare. His name was Hammy Sparks and, like a great many among the Ffestiniog train and engine crews, he was a volunteer. Sparks crooned the Welsh and English station names in a melodious, resonant baritone.

"Sounds Welsh," he said when I asked him about this idiosyncratic practice, "but it's not, I'm afraid. The singing was my own idea. The passengers seem to like it."

Among the Welsh narrow gauges, the Ffestiniog is the oldest, longest, and busiest. The 14-mile railway was established by an act of Parliament in 1832 to run from the slate quarries at Blaenau Ffestiniog down to the sea at Porthmadog. Steam engines replaced horses in 1863, though loaded slate wagons

Singing guard Hammy Sparks gives the driver a go-ahead.

continued to roll downgrade propelled only by gravity until World War II. (Originally the horses would ride down in special "dandy wagons.") Passenger service was inaugurated in 1865, roughly two years ahead of the Talyllyn, making it the first narrow-gauge passenger-hauling railway in Great Britain—and perhaps the world.

The slate business petered out in time, causing the railroad's closure in 1946, but preservationists—perhaps inspired by the success of their nearby Talyllyn counterparts—came to the rescue and, beginning in 1955, gradually reopened the line. This process came to a remarkable conclusion in 1982 when the upper 4 miles, which had been removed after the line's closure to make way for a power-generation reservoir, were relocated and rebuilt. It was this, of course, that made possible my circle journey by restoring the Ffestiniog Railway's northeastern connection with British Rail's Conwy Valley Line. To accomplish it, the "Deviationists," as the vol-

unteers responsible proudly called themselves, had to bore a substantial tunnel.

Like the Talyllyn, the Ffestiniog Railway was all about slate. Along the line I'd seen evidence of it: in dry walls, fences, houses. Now, as the train approached Blaenau Ffestiniog, I entered the mother lode of slate, a seemingly mystical world in shades of gray made all the grayer by the day's deep overcast. Mountains of slate rubble were everywhere. We rolled between buildings all of slate, surrounded by slate walls—far more walls than any town could need. It was as if Blaenau Ffestiniog was saddled with an historical imperative to consume slate.

Drab and monochromatic as it was, it seemed an appropriate Ultima Thule, "furthest north" for my slim-gauge journey—though my circle had many standard-gauge miles to go before I reached home base, Shrewsbury.

At Blaenau Ffestiniog, the end of the line and interchange with British Rail, *Blanche* can be seen from the observation car running around its train for the return journey to Harbour Station.

Amid the vastness of Patagonia, the Esquel Branch
mixed train chugs north toward El Maitén. (ABOVE)

The *machinista*, or engineer, on the Esquel Branch
looks as much like a gaucho as a railroader. (BELOW)

THE OLD PATAGONIAN EXPRESS

AGAINST A BACKDROP OF SNOW-CAPPED MOUNTAINS, NARROW ribbons of rail swung through parched hills covered with scrub vegetation. Little Mikados, some of them Baldwin products, American, some German Henschels, powered trains of wooden coaches and outside-braced boxcars on what could have been the Colorado narrow-gauge network or perhaps Southern Pacific's Keeler Branch. But it was 1988, not 1938, or '48, or '58, and this was the Esquel Branch in southern Argentina. On it traveled "the Old Patagonian Express," as Paul Theroux dubbed its mixed train in his 1978 travel memoir with that title. To locals, this frail convey-ance was affectionately called just *La Trochita,* the little narrow-gauge train.

Nestled in the foothills of the Andes, deep in the region that is known as Patagonia, between those mountains and the Atlantic Ocean, Esquel was a plain, workaday town when I visited, just beginning to gain some notoriety as a resort for skiing, fishing, and hiking. Yet this attractively unpretentious spot was not without a distinction. It was the southernmost point in South America linked by contiguous rail to the rest of the continent's system. The railway—75-centimeter-gauge (approximately 2 feet 6 inches) and 100 per-cent steam-powered—was a branch of the Ferrocarril General Roca, one of six state-owned companies created in 1948 when President Juan Perón nationalized the railroads as the Ferrocarril Argentinos. (General Julio Argentino Roca, the railway's namesake, had also been president of Argentina, twice.)

From Esquel, the slim-gauge branch stretched 249 miles north, generally within sight of the Andes, to Ingeniero Jacobacci, on the broad-gauge (5-foot 6-inch, sometimes called "Indian gauge") main line from the resort city of San Carlos de Bariloche—perched on the southeastern shore of Lago Nahuel Huap—to Buenos Aires. Twice-weekly mixed trains plied the Esquel Branch, connecting with the *Lagos del Sur*—which translates to "Lakes of the South," meaning those that surround Bariloche—on the broad gauge, a substantial, more modern train with sleepers and a diner. In addition to the scheduled mixed trains on the narrow gauge, charters exploited the line's nostalgic charms. On a chilly but bright April morning, I stood on the platform in Esquel, waiting to board just such a special train, which I would ride halfway up the branch, to the headquarters town of El Maitén. After spending the night there, I'd continue on the mixed north to Jacobacci, where I'd board the *Lagos del Sur* for Buenos Aires, a rail journey of 1,328 miles all told.

Before leaving Esquel on this April morning, fresh from a comfortable night at the Hotel Sol del Sur, our congenial group of 11 posed for a portrait on the platform. We ranged from those obsessed with steam locomotives—Gary Hunter, a highway engineer, his father, Don, a retired AV specialist from the University of Oregon, Rich Thom, an engineer-turned-manager from Santa Barbara, and me—to the more easygoing, including Marty Banks, a conductor on the Union Pacific, Dina and Phil Goldman from New Zealand and Dina's sister Bunty, and Gordon and Manetta Bennett. A member of a railroad museum in California, Gordon left buttons with its logo pinned to railroaders' caps throughout Argentina. Taking our picture was Chris Skow, the tour's organizer and veteran by then of some 20 rail trips to South America dating back in 1974. With us in the photo was Sergio Pastime, our Argentine guide, who hurdled the language barrier for us. Also included was one of the mugging little local boys who seemed drawn, as if by magic, to the lens-end of any camera.

We stood stiffly and smiled in front of our steam locomotive, No. 107, a 2-8-2 built in 1922 by Henschel & Sohn, a German company. Behind it were coupled a boxcar, a crew car, and *primera clase* (first-class) coach No. 1125, all built in 1922, in Belgium. An oval builder's plate on the coach's step read "*Societe Anonyme des Ateliers de Constructions de et a Familleureux*"—quite a mouthful, which could be translated as simply "the Familleureux workshops." At the end of the train was a wooden diner of indeterminate age and homespun ambiance, perhaps a product of the railroad's own shops in El Maitén

Esquel is the southernmost point connected to South America's rail network.

(where, I was told, it had been rebuilt just five years earlier) or of the General Roca shops in Buenos Aires.

Under a wide-brimmed leather hat, our engineer—or *machinista,* as he was called in Spanish—looked more like a *gaucho* than a railroader. He grabbed 107's whistle cord and, with two hoots, sent us scrambling back to board the train. In the pure sunshine of early morning, we lurched into motion, chuffing out of the station and past the small shops and "armstrong" turntable, where just a few minutes earlier we had watched one man turn our locomotive using just his sturdy back and strong legs. We whistled our way out of Esquel, climbing along rock ledges still deep in cool shade. Across the valley the mountain peaks dusted with snow were hardly higher than we. The morning had the crisp clarity of late fall, with more than slight intimations of the winter near at hand. The warmth pulsing from the coal stove at the coach's center was welcome.

On the valley floor the Lombardy poplars had turned a soft yellow. I watched the shadow of our train—the unmistakable silhouette of a steam locomotive, with its dancing smoke plume—flit across fields where sheep

Double-headed Henschels pose in the *Corte Blanco,* the "White Cutting," with the Esquel-bound special. The crew looms large in the cab of this tiny locomotive.

grazed. Holding tight to the handrail, I stood on the coach's gyrating open platform and listened to the stack talk as the train worked upgrade. We had been given the run of our charter train, to a degree both mind-boggling and liberating to *Norteamericanos* used to a hyper-cautious and litigious society (where, for example, Amtrak passengers have at times been instructed to remain seated until their train has come to a complete stop). We could sit or stand on the coaches' open platforms. We could ride on the roofs of the cars or in the locomotive cab or on the tender.

The previous day our southbound charter had been doubleheaded. Late in the afternoon, with the train stopped so the locomotive could take on water, Rich Thom and I had climbed up on the tender of the first engine. This was a potentially messy business; because all the engines on the Esquel Branch are oil-burners, their tenders typically are encrusted in bunker-C: slippery, staining, nasty stuff. Gary Hunter had picked up so much black goo on the seat of his jeans while tender-riding that for days he carried around a piece of plastic to sit on, lest he leave his mark in hotels and restaurants.

Rich and I had been perched just a few feet away from the tapered stack and rusted smokebox of the second engine. Once they got a roll on their train, both locomotives pounded out a cacophony of exhaust. We were engulfed in sound: a raging, clamoring roar. Black smoke poured from both stacks and, fortunately, was blown aside by a considerable wind. That chill wind buffeted us, and our faces were occasionally stung by sprinkles of light rain. The scene all around was dazzling: the hills and valley flashing yellow-brown in late sun, the Andes crowned in snow, and above them great puffs of white cumulous clouds darkening to gray. Our world was exhilaratingly fluid, with clouds blowing and turning sunshine to showers in an instant, and the tender dancing underfoot, really rocking at the 35 mph or so that we were making.

Cold, loud, uncomfortable, even a little frightening, this was an experience that hammered relentlessly at all the senses. It was indescribably invigorating. Looking over the lead locomotive's domes and stack as we swung around a curve, we saw a horse frozen with fear on the tracks. He stood there, head high, staring at the train, while the machinista sounded the whistle in urgent staccato blasts. Finally the horse turned, eased down the embankment, and galloped across the field with an equine grace all the more beautiful for having been endangered. Not long after that our train had eased to a stop. The portly, friendly *machinista* leaned his considerable bulk out the cab window and gestured questioningly. We nodded, then climbed down off the tender and up into the warm embrace of the locomotive cab, where we rode cozily for the remaining miles into Esquel.

The boiler's backhead was primitive, simple. The glassless pressure gauge, its numerals painted by hand, showed that we were running at about 150 pounds per square inch. The engineer pushed the throttle, levered from the middle of the backhead, with his foot. He effectively drove with the Johnson bar, or reversing lever, rather than making fine adjustments with the throttle. He applied the vacuum brakes with little taps on the handle.

Now northbound the following day, our charter train traipsed through mile after mile of country remarkably reminiscent of the North American West: barren brown hills where sheep and cattle grazed, backed by soaring mountains. We saw precious little sign of human habitation, which is why the little railroad had survived, an anachronism passed over by the forces of progress. Its history is obscure, perplexing, hard in some respects to pin down, and—given the apparent antiquity of its equipment and modus operandi—surprisingly recent and, in terms of its years of operations, surprisingly short.

Not completed until 1942, the Esquel Branch was originally planned as part of an extensive complex of narrow-gauge lines crisscrossing Argentine Patagonia. (Patagonia encompasses the southern reaches of Chile as well as Argentina.) The Patagonian Light Railways Network, which in retrospect seems a mad scheme, was planned by the government in the 1920s but for the most part was never completed. The 23 locomotives that had been recently active at the time of my 1988 visit (all Mikados, 13 inside-frame Henschels and 10 outside-frame Baldwins) and most of the freight and passenger cars then on the property dated from 1922 as part of this project. Astonishingly, the original order was for 81 locomotives, 50 2-8-2s from Henschel and 25 from Baldwin—plus, also from Henschel, 4 0-6-0T's and 2 0-8-0CT's, curious little tank engines with cranes plopped down on their boilers. The order to Belgium's Familleureux for rolling stock was for 25 first-class coaches and 25 second-class; 200 stock cars, 100 for cattle and 100 for sheep; 50 box cars; 70 tank cars, 35 for oil and 35 for water; 150 gondolas; and 230 flat cars.

The first step in the Argentine government's plan for the Patagonian Light Railways Network was to take over the British-built and -owned meter-gauge Central Chubut, a railway that dated from 1889 and ran from Puerto Madryn, on the Atlantic Coast some 1,000 miles south of Buenos Aries, to Trelew and Dolavon, in the interior. The grand project of a Patagonian rail system never got beyond a short extension of the Central Chubut and the eventual completion, after reroutings and construction in fits and starts, of the Esquel Branch.

Actually, the Esquel Branch's history can be traced back even further than the Patagonian Light Railways Network, to Law 5559, promoted by Minister Ramos Mexía and passed in 1908 by the Argentine Congress to develop the National Territories, including Patagonia. Broad-gauge rails were to spread through the region like veins of a leaf, part of a plan to sell government-owned land adjacent to the railways and populate the region—a model that had worked well in the western United States. In 1912, considerable expansion of the original network—including a line from the port city of Rio Gallegos to the Chilean border, with a branch to Rio Turbio—was proposed, but Mexía's resignation the following year and then World War I brought the plans for even the first phase to a halt well short of completion. (The last piece of this plan to be realized was the line to Bariloche, opened in 1934.) The success of narrow-gauge lines in Europe during the war, and the weakness of the Argentine economy after it, made a virtue of necessity: the "developmental railways" in Patagonia would be built in 75-centimeter gauge.

Marginal for years, the Esquel Branch apparently was a robust freight hauler in its heyday. By the time I rode, however, *La Trochita* had been increasingly buffeted, and service was down to just mixed trains in both directions on Sundays and Thursdays, plus the occasional freight. Not long before, the government had introduced buses between points served by the railway—in addition to the trains. But the locals, who took fierce pride in their railway and, probably accurately, figured that if the buses succeeded the trains would go, simply boycotted the buses. The buses disappeared and the trains rolled on, at least for a time, although freight business had dwindled to next to nothing. For some years the mixeds had journeyed mostly after dark, but in 1988 their schedule had been flopped (along with that of the *Lagos del Sur,* probably the dog that wagged the tail of the Esquel Branch change), yielding daylight timings. This was much more congenial to photography and sightseeing and surely was my good luck.

Dining on rails is always a special pleasure, but I hadn't counted on much in this department aboard *La Trochita.* Box lunches perhaps. But I'd been most pleasantly surprised. Entering the diner (its very presence unexpected) for lunch, we found the car's six tables for two (just enough for our group) laid with white linen. On each table stood bottles of red and white wine, beer, and Coca-Cola from which to choose. Our waiter wore a powder blue jacket and black bow tie. His wife cooked in the tiny galley. The first course was pea soup, followed by grilled mutton, peaches with custard and *dulce de leche,* and coffee. It was a remarkable meal, really, considering where we were and that we were traveling on rails about half the width of standard gauge. Nowhere more forcefully than in the diner was I reminded that these trains were small and carried with them the charm and wonder of things diminutive.

And all this in the face of the vast, lonely emptiness through which the Esquel Branch runs. The stations, with water towers (the locomotives had a seemingly insatiable thirst that required frequent stops to slake) and in some cases log houses for the section workers who maintained the line, were isolated oases of human life in a land otherwise belonging to sheep, cattle, horses, jackrabbits, and an array of birds. Of all the fragile settlements where we paused, Leleque was my favorite, hands down. A row of golden poplars lined the track, and through them I could see the workers' cabins, where a woman held up her young son to look at the train. Just beyond the water tank was the depot, also of log construction but whitewashed and trimmed in light blue. The door to the office was open, so I walked in and came across a curious device that I knew I recognized but hadn't seen for some time. Vanished from the United States railroad scene for as many decades as the steam locomotive, the telegraph was once essential to the movement of trains, and there in front of me was a key and a sounder that might clatter to life at any moment, speaking Morse in Spanish.

At photo runbys, where we all climbed down and unlimbered our cameras, the *machinista* hollered loud with the whistle, and the fireman—the

Old technologies, most notably telegraphy, are in
evidence on the desk of the station at Leleque.

foguista—stoked furiously to create dramatic smoke effects. *"Mucho fumar,"*
one of the crew said, grinning giddily.

In late afternoon we detrained at El Maitén, and from there most of the
group departed by van for the luxuries of a resort hotel in Bariloche, a few
hours distant. Gary, Don, Marty, Rich, and I elected to remain overnight in
El Maitén, however, to photograph the northbound *mixto,* train 1622, arriving
there from Esquel in early afternoon; three of us would then take it north to
Jacobacci, while the Hunters drove back to Bariloche. We put up at Hotel Ac-
comazzo, our only choice, bunking in one double and one triple room—at the
cost of 20 australs (the Argentine currency at the time) apiece, or about $3.25.
Dinner, served in a space that was also the bar and TV room, included a crepe
filled with ham, lettuce, and mayonnaise as a starter; a tasty noodle soup; and
chicken fried steak, all accompanied by a soccer match that screamed from
the TV. The only heat in the establishment was a huge fireplace in this dining
room, and nights are crisp in El Maitén, even in the fall.

The following afternoon the mixed from Esquel arrived shortly after one o'clock—nearly on time—and there was considerable bustle on the platform at El Maitén as departure for Jacobacci neared. Friends and family members swirled around, saying farewell to travelers. Locomotives were traded, since the north end of the line was operated by Baldwins (their shorter wheelbases better suited to that section of the branch's tighter curves), while the Henschels worked to the south. The stationmaster rang the depot bell. Now in charge, outside-frame Mikado No. 5 whistled off with a heavy train of nine cars in tow: two tank cars, two boxcars, a railroad office car, our diner from the day before, a *primera clase* coach, a *segundo clase* coach, and a crew car.

Leaving town, the train rolled past the shop building where the equipment for the branch was maintained. Two days earlier we'd visited the shops and watched a pair of locomotives being rebuilt, a Baldwin and a Henschel. On the woodworking side, using hand tools such as saws and files, carpenters painstakingly renovated a pair of second-class wooden coaches. One was nearly finished and painted, the other little more than a skeleton of raw wood. Poking around the yard, we'd found a switch stand lettered, "Ramapo Iron Works, Hillburn, N.Y." The earliest patent date was October 19, 1897.

Although the mixed was nearly full, we found seats in the *primera*, where most of the generally well dressed passengers seemed to know one another. Built in Buenos Aires in 1960, the car was comfortable enough, with soft walkover seats and shuttered windows. It was alive with the murmur of Spanish. "*Claro, claro,*" one woman repeated, but nothing at all was clear to me. An elderly couple shared *maté,* the national drink of Argentina, a strong tea sipped from a gourd. In the second-class coach, the scene was dramatically different, looking as though the passengers were camping out around the stove at the car's center. Some sprawled on the hard wooden seats, while others lay crosswise on the floor, trying to sleep—and blocking the aisle. Wood scraps littered the floor.

North from El Maitén lay hours of unrelieved upgrade. Beyond Fitalancao, a water stop, the tracks made a particularly steep, looping scramble up the hillside. As we doubled back, I could look straight down and see the water tank and station far below. With the afternoon sun comfortably warm on my face, I sat on the steps of the open platform. I watched and listened as the Baldwin labored mightily to keep us moving. The train slowed to a walk; actually, it was a nearly (but not quite) irresistible temptation to hop down to the ground and jog alongside the coach, keeping pace. The locomotive's exhaust became so measured that it seemed we'd stall—and then what? A black tower of smoke marked our passing as the foguista poured on the oil. High atop a ridge ahead, two gauchos on horseback were silhouetted against a dramatic sky. Perfectly still and remote, they stood watching—perhaps to see if we'd make it.

The *Viejo Expreso Patagonico,* the Spanish rendering
of the name Paul Theroux gave the Esquel Branch
mixed, struggles upgrade from Norquinco.

We did. In celebration, Rich, Marty, and I went to the diner for a glass of
Schneider beer. The car jostled and rattled soothingly, growing dimmer inside
as dusk fell and the last stain of pink-purple faded from the horizon. Amid the
savory smells of meat cooking, we drank a second beer. Over the doorway at
one end of the car, a crucifix swayed. The same waiter had served us the day
before on the charter; since the railroad rostered only a single diner, perhaps
they needed only one waiter. He invited us into the kitchen to wash up; his
wife handed us soap and a towel. We were the only customers that night, but
we enjoyed our asparagus soup, chicken-fried steak with a fried egg, French
fries, *vino tinto,* pudding, and coffee. The dinner cost us each 30 australs,
about $4.25, including the wine. The waiter appeared to say we could eat all
we wanted, since he'd laid on food for a full car.

Walking back to our coach, we paused a moment on the open platform
and looked at a sky teeming with fiercely bright stars. A crescent moon hung

to the west. The Milky Way seemed almost palpable. Rich pointed out the Southern Cross, a constellation to which I'd been a stranger. Ahead, billows of white smoke piled high as our Mike soldiered on, leading its archaic train through the empty reaches of Patagonia. Orange flashes from the firebox flitted across the landscape and illuminated the embracing wreaths of steam. The locomotive's headlight cut a white swath as the train swung around curve after curve. We were finally driven inside by the frigid air. The handrails were almost too cold to hold.

When Paul Theroux rode the Esquel Branch mixed to end his journey from Boston, made mostly by rail and chronicled in *The Old Patagonian Express*, he found the trip somewhat boring, the coaches dirty, and the locomotive "a kind of demented samovar on wheels." (About that he had a point.) He was on the last lap of his trek and eager for it to end. I, on the other hand, felt sure my Esquel Branch journey was one I'd never forget.

For the final miles into Jacobacci (the very last bit over dual-gauge track), conversation clustered around the coach's silver-painted stove, as it might have in an old-fashioned general store. Rails grumbled below, the wooden car creaked, and the windows rattled in their frames. Muted voices ebbed and flowed in the dim light. A mother pulled her sleeping son onto her lap and hugged him. We dozed, happy for the peace and warmth, in no rush to move on to the next stage of our journey.

Photo runby at Ingeniero Atilo Cappa. (ABOVE)

Ferrocarril Industrial Rio Turbio's Mitsubishi-built 2-10-2 poses in the late sun. (BELOW)

6

RIO TURBIO, COAL HAULER

E ARLY MORNING, APRIL 15, 1988. IN DEEPEST PATAGONIA, THE Argentine port city of Rio Gallegos was foggy and overcast, dank with swirling mists from the nearby Atlantic. In this chill, gray murk, the haloed headlight of low-slung 2-10-2 No. 114 glowed. Above the soft hiss of steam and the whine of a turbogenerator, voices called commands in Spanish.

Behind the Santa Fe and its auxiliary water car were four wooden coaches—the chartered train that I'd soon be riding—all wearing a jazzy paint scheme of bright orange with blue stripes, a modernistic aesthetic that belied the cars' antiquity. Coal smoke poured from four smoke jacks, promising a welcome warmth aboard these jaunty cars. Crew and officials bustled about the little train as 9 AM departure drew near for an all-day charter that would run the full 160-mile length of this coal-hauling railroad to the mines at Rio Turbio, in the foothills of the Andes.

Then the southernmost railroad in the world and 100 percent steam powered, the Ferrocarril Industrial Rio Turbio stretched east-west across the southern tip of Argentina, some 1,650 miles from the capital city of Buenos Aires. Built by the Argentine government to the unusual gauge of 75 centimeters, the line was opened in 1951. When I visited, it was operated by Yacimientos Carboniferos Fiscales—the Argentine Coal Board—to haul low-grade coal from the mines at Rio Turbio to the port city of Rio Gallegos, where it was transloaded to YCF's own ships. At Buenos Aires, the Rio Turbio coal was mixed with high-grade imported coal for burning at electric power stations.

Although coal is not plentiful in Argentina, the Rio Turbio fields were sufficiently remote that, in spite of their discovery before the turn of the last century, serious thought of exploitation didn't begin until the 1940s. To get the coal to tidewater, the first surveys projected a railway line terminating at Santa Cruz, an established Atlantic port about 150 miles north of Rio Gallegos. However, the final plan, adopted in 1949, called for a line 86 miles shorter with far easier grades, achieved by following the Rios Turbio and Gallegos. The hurdle was building a new port at the estuary of the Rio Gallegos, where spring tide was an incredible 52 feet higher than ebb.

If proximity and moderation of gradient dictated the route, gauge was determined by historical accident. Most of the vast over-order for 75 2-8-2's delivered in 1922 for the Patagonian Light Railway Network ended up on the Esquel Branch, but more than enough locomotives and material were left over to open the Rio Turbio line as well some three decades later, and 75-centimeter gauge was selected in order to make use of these surpluses. Thus the Rio Turbio's first locomotives were eight Henschel 2-8-2's, sisters to those that plied the Esquel Branch. These Henschels were quickly replaced, however, because they were inadequately powerful for a railroad that—in spite of its diminutive gauge, halfway between the Maine 2-footers and the 3-foot-wide Colorado narrow gauge—was a relatively big-time, high-volume coal hauler. From Japan's Mitsubishi in 1956, therefore, came ten 2-10-2's, followed by another ten essentially identical locomotives in 1963. It was this fleet of Santa Fes that I discovered when I arrived in Rio Gallegos in 1988.

By the morning of our charter, organized by Chris Skow's Trains Unlimited Tours, our little band of a dozen steam-locomotive aficionados had already been in Rio Gallegos two nights. We'd put up at the pleasantly plain Hotel Alonso—"35 *habitaciones con bano privado.*" From our rooms we could clearly hear the little 2-10-2's whistling for a road crossing near the shops, just a few blocks away.

Rio Gallegos was a raw, tough, two-story town of broad streets, reminiscent of the energy boom towns of the American West. It seemed appropriate that Butch Cassidy and the Sundance Kid had robbed the Banco de Londres y Tarapaca in Rio Gallegos in 1905. I went down to the engine terminal my first night in town. In front of a substantial four-track, corrugated-metal enginehouse, five 2-10-2's steamed quietly. Contours of boilers and angularities of machinery were highlighted by the incandescent light spilling through the open doors of the engine shed. The rich smell of coal smoke laced the chill evening air, and cinders crunched underfoot. Inside, big barrel stoves radiated a cozy heat that drew me back every little while from my outdoor wanderings. On a wall in the back corner of the shop was a large chart listing the current status of the Santa Fe's, Nos. 101–120, all of them modern and stoker-fired.

At 10 PM a whistle wailed in the distance, announcing the arrival of a loaded coal train at a road crossing on the outskirts of town. A few minutes later a headlight flared down the tracks, and I heard then rapid, soft exhaust of what turned out to be No. 110 breezing into town with about 875 tons of coal strung out behind its auxiliary tender. The Santa Fe worked steam on past the road crossing by the shops, pulling the loads into the clear. The little 2-10-2 left the cars in two cuts, to be run through the dumper the next day. There the coal would be added to the huge mountain already stockpiled for transloading by conveyor belt to a ship.

His evening's work done, the engineer, bathed in the yellow glow of the cab lights, spun the twin-handled reversing wheel, then hauled abruptly out on the throttle. As the 2-10-2 scooted backward past the crew shack, the fireman unloaded, skipping along as he hit the ground with scoop and satchel in hand. I walked back to the Alonso through air heavy with the fragrances of coal smoke and the sea.

At the engine terminal the next morning, locomotives bustled here and there under great billows of steam silhouetted against a cobalt-blue Patagonian sky. The early-morning sun washed with gold the engines' remarkably low (just 2 feet 9½ inches in diameter) red-spoked drivers and Walschaerts valve gear. But the morning's brightness and the enginehouse activity belied the fact that we were caught in a downward spiral of diminishing prospects. In had begun three days earlier in Buenos Aires, when Segio Pastime, the languidly Latin artist who was serving as our "native guide," helping with language problems and dealing with local customs, gave us some bad news.

"We have a problem," he'd said. "There will be a general strike on Thursday." Not only would this force a rescheduling of our two-day charter trip. It was sure to cut at least in half the number of coal trains we could expect to see, since on one of our two days in Rio Gallegos there would be absolutely no activity. To make matters worse, on the evening of our arrival we had learned that, for the following day, the usual schedule of two trains daily in each direction would be reduced to one as the mine geared down for the strike. The spiral tightened again the next morning when we got the news that a conveyor belt at the mine had broken, so no empties or loads at all would be moving that day.

Apparently, all the engine-terminal activity was in preparation for two days of hibernation, not work. Still, it was a fine show as the steamers darted about, heading for the chute that provided coal for the engines from the same massive stash that filled the ships' holds; paused over ash pits so that fires could be cleaned and banked; and reshuffled themselves on the ready tracks into a priority order by no means clear to the visitor. Then at noon came the first good news in days. FIRT operating officials, sorry about our disappointment over the cancelled coal trains, decided to dispatch a train of empties to a passing siding 32 miles up the line just for our benefit. So at noon No. 104 headed out of town under darkening skies with 51 empties in tow (the typical length of a Rio Turbio train) for Kilometer 52. Our entire group of 12, along with our leaders, Sergio and Chris, watched the empties rattle across the last grade crossing in Rio Gallegos. Then most of the group headed for Lago Argentino's spectacular glaciers, leaving just three of us to pace 104 in a rented car.

My companions were Gary Hunter and his father, Don, 73 years old and game for anything (including riding on tenders and boxcar roofs). Slight, short, but rugged, with a graying dark beard and a lively, open face, Gary was a highway engineer whose intensive summer work season left him plenty of time off during the rest of the year to travel to Africa and Central America frequently, among other destinations. On the other hand, this was the first international venture for Don, a retired audiovisual director from the University of Oregon. Using the elaborate, cumbersome, homemade equipment required in the pioneering days of electronics, Don had set out in the 1940s to make disk recordings of vanishing sounds such as trolley cars clanging by. Though not at the time a railfan, he had gone to Cajon Pass to record Southern Pacific's cab-forwards but, due to a washout, had seen only a light helper move. In the years following that disappointment, Don would tape countless hours of steam locomotive sounds. Rarely did a locomotive turn a wheel on the Rio Turbio without Don's microphone pointed in its direction.

Back in Rio Gallegos, we explored the rotary dumpers. Although then sitting silent, in a few days they would again resound with the shrieking of metal on metal and the roar of coal cascading out of capsized gondolas. We moved on to the Quonset hut where heavy locomotive repairs were made. No. 107 stood driverless on jacks over the pit, shining in fresh paint: black trimmed in red, with the cab lined out in blue and white. On the floor nearby were its newly turned drivers, the middle set "blind," flangeless; this allowed the locomotive, with its long wheelbase, to squeeze around the railroad's tight curves—an accommodation I expected to see on model railroads, but not on prototype pikes. Apparently the 107 once had been wrecked; a small plaque on the cab side read, "*Reconstruida* 1987."

Outside, we were looking over the circular brick firepit where drivers were heated to remove or replace tires when a frantically shrill police whistle heralded the arrival of a wildly gesticulating watchman. We handed him the FIRT general manager's business card, which we'd been given as credentials when we arrived. This worked, and the watchman became effusively friendly.

Still under steam, the YCF tug Enrique awaits a rising tide
at Rio Gallegos. (ABOVE LEFT)

The watchman at Rio Gallegos poses with his catch. (ABOVE RIGHT)

Don also gave him his own business card, with a beautiful photo he had taken
of Southern Pacific 4449 charging along in *Daylight* dress. Arms gyrating like
pistons and side rods, the watchman was clearly asking "How fast?" When
Don punched "80" into his pocket calculator for conversion from miles to
kilometers per hour, "129" popped up. With a rueful smile, the watchman
pointed at the 107, drew a "60" in the cinders, and shrugged.

After taking us through the company's electric generating station (coal-
powered steam turbines, predictably) our new friend brought us to his kiosk,
where he grabbed a string of fish he had caught that day and showed them off
with a broad, proud grin. One of the engine terminal's charms was its proximity to the river. The water, or what there was of it at low tide, was right there,
and we could see the YCF collier (with blue-and-white funnel markings) atilt,
snuggled into the riverbed at its pier. Not far away, YCF's handsome steam
tug *Enrique* sat high and dry in the middle of a mud flat. Wisps of coal smoke
coiled from its tall stack as the boat awaited the flood tide that would allow

it to go back to work. We whiled away the next day with a visit to a penguin colony at Cape Virgenes, 87 miles distant on a gravel road overlaid with a gumbo of wet clay. Our charter to Rio Turbio left the day after that.

The appearance that morning of 114, the power for our train, was not an unqualified hit. When we'd seen it switching on our first afternoon in town, it had looked like a typical road-weathered coal hauler, but now it was thoroughly duded up. Rods and drivers were painted in red and outlined in white, along with anything else that could conceivably be trimmed in ether of these colors. The most controversial decoration was a huge blue-and-white (the colors of the Argentine flag) bull's-eye target that virtually covered the locomotive's smokebox. This disk, Chris was quick to point out when some of us grumbled, was similar to ones once carried by steam locomotives of the General Belgrano Railway in northern Argentina. (To further the analogy, the Mitsubishi Santa Fes were modeled on the Belgrano's class E2 2-10-2's.)

Nor were the coaches a vision of traditionalism, what with their bright orange livery, although under their paint they were wooden classics, dating from 1922 and acquired from the General Roca at El Maitén for just such charters as ours. They were not, of course, workaday equipment, since hauling passengers was not a regular occurrence on the Rio Turbio. But overriding all of this, in retrospect at least, was the fact that the decoration was done in the spirit of festivity and with a great deal of pride.

Front to back, beginning behind 114's auxiliary tender, the consist was 102, a coach included for employees, their families, and others, looking inside much as it did when built as part of the Patagonian Railways' equipment order; 4103, a coach with a bar added at one end and reclining seats from some standard-gauge chair car installed, a single pair across, in place of the original 2-and-1 seating; and 4102 and 4101, two coaches turned into business cars with berths and seating in lounge areas. No. 4101, which brought up the rear, had broad picture windows that were splendid for viewing, although they gave the car a somewhat anomalous appearance from outside.

At 9:15 AM, after an emergency air-line replacement, we whistled off on our strike-delayed departure into the misty desolation of Patagonia. During our all-day journey, we would see scant evidence of human habitation—just occasional railroad buildings, a few small villages, and *estancias*, ranches. For the first hour or so, we beat our way across a flat, treeless emptiness, the landscape most associated with Patagonia. Then, about the same time the clouds began to break up, we entered the valley of the Rio Gallegos and the countryside suddenly began to change character. Standing out on the open platform with the warm sun on my face, I saw vistas typical of the American West unfold as we steamed along: rolling yellow-brown hills covered with scrub vegetation, a snaking blue river, a sky scattered with puffy cumulus clouds.

Cab rides were available. Taking advantage of that, I climbed up and shook hands with our *machinista,* a portly gentleman sporting a bushy, droopy mustache, and his *foguista.* With a tug on the whistle cord and a hand on the throttle, the engineer launched our little train into motion. We moved up to a cruising speed near 40 mph, substantially greater than the 20 to 25 mph standard for the coal trains, with little effort. The Mitsubishi's tiny drivers spun in wild, unaccustomed liberation.

The tender apron was a surprisingly stable perch from which to survey the cab. The counterweighted firebox door was cracked just enough for me to see the flames leap and the coal being sprayed as the fireman adjusted the stoker valve. He used his scoop to tuck coal into the near corners of the firebox that the stoker didn't hit. Boiler pressure hovered around 170 to 175 psi. Before long, the fireman invited me to take his seat; from there I watched startled ostriches zigzag away with their comic gait and pink flamingos explode red into flight from the smooth surface of the Rio Gallegos. Soon it was time for *maté*—the strong green tea generally sipped from a gourd through a metal straw. Aboard No. 114, the gourd was replaced by a tin pot, kept hot on the backhead shelf. Engineer and fireman passed it back and forth, then included me in the circle, one after another sipping the pungent leafy brew, a ritual of hospitality that warmed me as much as the tea did.

We stopped for lunch at Ingeniero Atilio Cappa, a small compound recently renamed to honor the man who chose the route along the Rio Gallegos and Rio Turbio for the railway. Ing. Cappa, the approximate midpoint on the line, included a modern dormitory for section workers and their families. In the lunchroom there we ate sandwiches and empanadas brought along on the train. After a photo runby, the 114 shuffled off with our train to the west end of the passing track, and before long a distant whistle announced No. 102's approach with downbound loads from the mine. The coal train slunk into the passing siding, wrapped around us, and clattered off to a water stop and crew change at Ing. Cappa.

During the final segment of our journey, the snow-capped Andes, not far to the southwest, glittered in the late sun. Trees began to appear, but they were blighted, ravaged specimens haunted by winds that rarely cease. As we rolled into Rio Turbio, I could see the adits off to the south of the tracks. Now about 5 miles long, these tunnels had bumped into the Chilean border. Negotiations to dig under Chilean territory had stalled, and for the time being at least, tunnels could only branch out laterally.

A gritty mining town, Rio Tubio was no-nonsense and short on amenities, but we were comfortable at the Automobile Club's motel, where the ashtrays

After completing a photo runby at Ingeniero Cappa,
No. 114 waits at the west end of the passing track
there to meet No. 112 with Rio Gallegos-bound coal.

read, "*Capital Nacional del Carbon.*" Dinner at a small, no-fuss, family-run *parilla,* or grillroom typical of Argentine restaurants, was a well-charred and chewy but tasty smorgasbord of meats, brought to our table on skewers.

But the best grill of all we had the following day on our return to Rio Gallegos. It came by serendipity, the best way of all, every venturesome traveler's hope. We were headed east under dreary skies behind Santa Fe 111, well weathered with road grime, not gussied-up. Again we stopped for lunch at Ing. Cappa, where Chris Skow, never bashful, put into effect a plan he'd been pondering. On the outbound journey, we'd noticed a fine-looking sheep ranch that was a handsome cluster of whitewashed buildings. With Sergio translating, Skow asked Stephen Tita, the amiable chief mechanical officer who was the ranking railroader on board, if he couldn't call ahead and arrange for us to visit. The response, I gathered, had something to do with a celebration.

Our train pulled into Bella Vista, a dot on the map with hardly any apparent habitations but one that at the moment was aswirl with perhaps 100 celebrants of all ages. They had gathered, we learned, to mark the twentieth anniversary of their school. Still looking good atop a slight rise, Escuela No. 37 was a small but proud structure that we could see across a sweep of field. And the townspeople were having fun. In full swing was an *asado,* a sort of circular, open-pit barbecue with half a dozen splayed lambs skewered on cross-shaped iron spits called *asadors* and grilling slowly and aromatically over smoldering embers.

Eaten on bread and liberally laced with a homemade sauce called *salmuera*—vinegar with garlic, chilies, and oregano—this mutton was succulent. It was pressed on our happily befuddled group with enthusiastic hospitality, as were wine and pieces of a cake (in the shape of the schoolhouse) that was cut to loud applause just after we arrived. Leading the welcoming committee were Alec and Jessie MacKenzie, who spoke elegant English with a Scots burr and whose ancestors came from the Isle of Lewis in the Hebrides. On all sides were handshakes, smiles, and conversations, some carried on in broken Spanish and energetic gesticulations. The day was alive with festive electricity, and the townspeople of Bella Vista no doubt thought it a good omen that a trainload of *Norteamericanos* had appeared as if fated for their celebration. We felt the good fortune to be all ours.

Warm, effervescent Gem James, daughter of the MacKenzies, with her Chilean husband, Roberto, managed Estancia Carlotta, just a few miles further down the rail line. So we piled on the train and, with Gem as our guide, whistled off amid much shouting and waving on both sides. There is, after all, no farewell quite like the final flourish from an open platform at train's end, a salute to rapidly shrinking figures left behind. A group of schoolchildren ran along the tracks after us, laughing and waving and calling out, saying goodbye and thanks for coming.

While No. 111 steamed softly, resting securely on the main line—it was Sunday, so no coal trains were scheduled, making the railroad ours alone— Gem and Roberto led us through the buildings of the expansive ranch, 65,000 hectares (160,618 acres) that were home to 25,000 sheep. We saw shearing barn, mess hall, greenhouse, the works, then accepted Gem's invitation to tea with the assembled family in her handsome, green-trimmed stucco house.

"Only in Patagonia," Jessie MacKenzie exclaimed with a laugh and a clap of the hands, commenting on this incongruous mixing of people from far-away places.

"Whiskey?" the white-jacketed steward aboard the train later asked me shyly, as afternoon fell into evening and we rattled our last miles back to Rio Gallegos. I thanked him and let the neat Scotch warm me. The bright incandescent lights brought out a luster in the coach's wood paneling invisible by day. Out the windows, a fiery sunset had dimmed to a slim streak of yellow in the northwest. The rails clamored, and coal smoke blew back. A peace suffused the coaches as we lurched rhythmically along. Heads nodded.

But No. 111's whistle shrilled, calling us back as it sent a warning to the vehicles on the first paved road we'd seen all day. Suddenly the spray of lights of Rio Gallegos was close ahead, then all around. Within minutes the adventure was over.

Stubby, mustachioed, rotund Mechanical Officer Tita shook hands all around. "You had a good time?" he asked, beaming.

the Southernmost Railway in the World

When I rode the Ferrocarril Industrial Rio Turbio, it had been the southernmost railway in the world, but no longer. Then the Ferrocarril Austral Fueguino, which bills itself as *El Tren del Fin del Mundo,* or "the end of the world train," opened in 1994—or reopened, depending on how you look at it—claiming (or reclaiming) that which had been its distinction when it first opened in 1909. Naturally, I wanted to ride the new record holder, and when Holland America Line's *Amsterdam* made a port call at Ushuaia with me aboard in March 2004, I seized the opportunity. I found that, though the Ferrocarril Austral Fueguino's main claim to fame is geographical, its size is hardly a less salient characteristic. It is less than 5 miles long and only about 2 feet wide.

Ushuaia itself is an extreme place. The capital of the Argentine island province of Tierra del Fuego, "land of fire," it calls itself the world's southernmost city, a claim that relies on the definition of "city"—big enough to disqualify the nearby Chilean island settlement of Puerto William, small enough to edge out the larger, more northerly Punta Arenas, also in Chile. Through the early years of the twentieth century, Ushuaia's focal point was the penal colony for serious criminals that Argentina established there, much as Britain had done in Australia. The prison was, in fact, the original reason for the railway.

"Looks like Thomas the Tank Engine," one train passenger said of *Camila,* our train's tiny steam locomotive, when we boarded at Estación Andén Parque Nacional, the west end of the line that would carry us through the Parque Nacional Tierra del Fuego. It was an apt comparison for this little outside-frame, oil-burning 2-6-2T, completed in Britain by Winson Engineering in 1995 in emulation of century-older motive power. I grabbed a seat in the first compartment of the first car, tiny but plush, so I was face to face through the front window with *Camila.* On the adjacent track I spotted what was then the line's only other active steam locomotive, a tiny version of the classic Beyer-Garratt design. Named *Ing.*

L. D Porta, it honored the Argentine engineer (1922–2003) who was perhaps the most noted late-era steam guru, whose forward-looking designs bid, though unsuccessfully, to create viable future for the steam locomotive. His namesake engine, completed in 1994, was the first steam locomotive ever built in Argentina.

Just before *Camila* announced our departure with shrill whistle blasts, Claudio de Souza slipped into the compartment with me. He was the railway's mechanical engineer, so I had my own personal guide.

"We're a small family company," he said of the current railroad. "We all do everything. The driver does maintenance, and sometimes I drive." From Claudio, and from the taped commentary that played almost constantly over the carriages' loudspeakers (competing too aggressively for my taste with the chugging and whistling of the locomotive, always music to my ears), I learned the railway's history. Known from the beginning as the "convict train," its primary function was to haul timber, used both for construction of the town and prison and as fuel at the prison. The railway was closed in 1952 and eventually torn up. Forty-two years later, it was relaid (in just slightly narrower gauge, 50 rather than 60 centimeters) and reopened to show tourists an inaccessible but scenic section of Tierra del Fuego National Park.

On its way to the Estación del Fin del Mundo—the end of the line for the moment, some 6 miles from Ushuaia—the train meanders along the Rio Pipo and across meadowlands strewn with gray, barkless stumps, a certain clue to the railway's original, somber purpose. Today, in dramatic contrast, it's all for fun.

At Estación del Fin del Mundo, *Camilia* runs around its train.

Outside-frame 2-8-0 No. 45 works upgrade toward
the Devil's Nose and Alausi. (ABOVE)

Consolidations meet at Ventuva, east of Bucay. No. 41 has
the Duran-bound mixed in tow. (BELOW)

7

SWITCHBACKS ON THE DEVIL'S NOSE

HROATY, SYNCOPATED SOUNDS OF STEAM-LOCOMOTIVE exhaust whispered in a predawn blackness that was just softening to blue, and pinpoints of yellow light danced like fireflies. On that warm June morning in Duran, the seaport terminus of Ecuador's narrow-gauge Guayaquil & Quito Railway, those fireflies were Adlake kerosene lanterns wielded by brakeman and conductor, bobbing instructions to the engineer. Backing his train, he leaned from the cab of No. 11, a trim, fetching Mogul-type steamer built in the United States by the Baldwin Locomotive Company in 1900.

In front of me stood a foursquare, concrete station of indeterminate age, ringed with red and blue stripes no doubt intended to lend an air of modernity; through an open window, in contrast, I heard the chatter of Morse code, still the communication lifeline of the G&Q. Behind me, propped up by a forest of thick bamboo poles, was the original wooden station, now sagging and derelict.

A final flurry of fireflies brought No. 11's train to a halt at the station platform. Two wooden clerestory coaches—"*primera clase,*" according to gold lettering on the cars' red sides—and a round-roofed baggage-mail car ("*equi-*

paje/correo") made up the modest train. The locomotive (in common with the rest of the G&Q's fleet of Baldwin steamers and Alco diesels), the style of the rolling stock, the lanterns, even the somewhat incongruous round can-style hats worn by conductor and brakeman, all were ghosts of traditional North American railroading. For while South America's railroads most often had been promoted by Europeans, the 281-mile, 3-foot 6-inch-gauge Guayaquil & Quito had been completed in 1908 by American interests, concluding some 37 years of often-interrupted construction.

No. 11's consist was a Trains Unlimited, Tours special, bound that day for the little town of Alausi, high in the Andes—a 12-hour, 89-mile trek, up sustained grades reaching 5.6 percent through a double switchback and around twin horseshoe curves. By evening I'd have traveled from sea level to 7,700 feet—and from 1989 back to the turn of the last century.

Both aspects of the journey would be striking, particularly since that all-day ascent had implications more complex than the merely geographic. With resonances of Ernest Hemingway's mountains and lowlands as moral metaphor, the passage would lift me and a small band of 13 likeminded fellow travelers from the squalid, rank, teeming, tropical poverty of Guayaquil to the cool Andean freshness of Alausi.

As the early morning brightened to gray, No. 11 steamed quietly, air pumps panting irregularly, like a bad heart, generator whining to keep headlight and cab lights a bright yellow-white. The surrounding streetscape that dawn focused out of the darkness was uninspiring. Duran, a "suburb" across the Rio Guayas from Guayaquil, made that gritty city look good, which was no mean feat.

Guayaquil is Ecuador's chief commercial city and seaport, notable in the late 1980s as home of perhaps the world's most active pirate bands, who routinely boarded and robbed container ships and other vessels entering the harbor. A highway bridge linked the city to Duran, but there was also a ferry, somehow truer to the karma of the place. Our group had used the ferry a few days earlier for a visit to the G&Q's locomotive and car shops in Duran.

We had boarded the *Azuay* under the rusty corrugated roof of the ferry shed in Guayaquil. Slums clung to the hills; some fine old buildings stood decaying; the *Maria,* a small coastwise freighter, listed forlornly in the brown harbor water. The smell of burning garbage hung in the air. Looking incongruously prosperous, a sleek jet knifed upward through the murk from the international airport where our Ladeco flight from Miami had set us down earlier in the day.

With the raspy roar of diesels, the crowded ferry beat eastward across the river. In a cage at the stern, the engineer slumped on his bench, a bare foot propped up on a table next to the controls. Shrill horn blasts from the wheelhouse gave him his instructions. In just a few minutes the workaday vessel bumped against the dock in Duran, and we were carried by the debarking throng across the gangway and into a world of steam railroading—to the natives mundane and ordinary, to us dreamlike and remarkable.

Long an operational adjunct of the railroad, a rail ferry across the Rio Guayas had in fact been stipulated in an 1897 contract between Ecuadorian president General Eloy Alfaro and Archer Harmon & Associates, the group of American capitalists who brought the Guayaquil & Quito Railway Company into being in its current dimensions. The contract also directed the American firm to push the often-stymied rail line through to Quito, Ecuador's capital high in the Andes; supply the rolling stock and motive power; build the stations; and operate the finished product—all of which explains the distinctly North American flavor that the railroad still retains.

When Señorita America Alfaro, Eloy's daughter, drove the ceremonial golden spike to complete the project on June 18, 1908 (Eloy's birthday), Guayaquil was finally linked to Quito, some 140 miles away as the crow flies but 281 miles by the railroad, a ratio that speaks eloquently of the difficulty of the engineering. When I visited, little enough had changed. With the exception of one critical section of line near the railroad's midpoint, obliterated in a landslide caused by El Niño floods roughly a decade before, the original route was intact. Of the eight 2-6-0's (Baldwin 1900–1901) around for the inauguration, three—Nos. 7, 11, and 14—remained in service.

The G&Q encompassed three divisions: the 55-mile Division Costa from Duran to Bucay, at the foot of the Andes; the 50-mile Division Montana to Riobamba; and the 183-mile Division Sierra to Quito. The oldest is the Coastal Section. The first piece of it, the 26 miles between Yaguachi and Barraganeta, was completed in 3-foot gauge by the government in 1874 with funds provided years earlier by a British loan; from the beginning this was seen as just one link in a chain that would eventually connect Guayaquil with Quito. Bucay was reached in 1884 and, in the other direction, Duran in 1888. But, except for some abortive attempts at grading into the Andes from Bucay, that was that.

Then, finally, President Alfaro's energetic focus on getting the railroad built came into happy correlation with the American capitalists' desire to build it, and the enterprise went forward at last. The Guayaquil & Quito Railway Company was incorporated in New Jersey, with an office in New York City. The existing Duran-Bucay trackage was widened from 3-foot gauge to 3 feet 6 inches. Some 3,000 Ecuadorian laborers, led by American engineers and foremen, under the direction of Archer Harmon's brother John, began in earnest the construction of what would be one of the most spectacular mountain railroads ever built.

This was the railroad that lay ahead of us as we awaited departure amid Duran's decrepitude, a sorry but not altogether inappropriate setting for the jewel that was No. 11, which itself showed the wear and tear of a long, hard life. Well-wiped boiler jacket and tender in yellow-lined red livery retained a faded elegance, though a patina of soot and oil (burned by all G&Q steamers) ensured a workaday mien. "*Reconstruida en Duran Ecuado Marzo* 1955" read the plate on No. 11's smokebox, recording a March 1955 rebuilding.

Our early exit was set to get us out of town before the 6:25 A M scheduled departure of the daily *mixto,* or mixed train, which backed in on the opposite side of the station while we waited. In charge was Alco diesel No. 161, one of a fleet of 10 that, when delivered to the G&Q in 1971, had virtually diesel-ized the railroad. In time, however, the units, built in Spain by Alco licensee Eskalduna, declined and deteriorated. Some were cannibalized to keep the strongest among them on the rails. In 1989, only four remained in service, two on the Duran end of the railroad and two on the Quito end. This meant that steam, once effectively reduced to yard service, had made a surprising comeback on both the Coast and Mountain Sections.

After a brief delay to repack one of the baggage car's journal boxes, we whistled off, pulling past a curious monument: a 2-foot-gauge 0-4-0 atop a high pedestal bearing the inscription "*homenaje al ferroviario*" (a tribute to the railway worker). Our wooden coach creaked and groaned as we lurched and swayed out of town, rolling by bits and pieces of derelict steamers that languished in the long grass. No. 11 worked easily as we rolled across lowlands scattered with bamboo shacks on stilts. In flooded rice paddies we saw grace-ful, long-necked white herons. We saw cattle grazing and a tickbird perched dutifully on a horse's back. A donkey charged down the road toward the tracks, dragging a small boy behind it.

We crossed the substantial Rio Yaguachi, then curved into its namesake town, where we met a Duran-bound workers' train from Milagro, a city a few miles further up the line. This was an *autoferro,* one of the ubiquitous white railcars with blue trim, most rebuilt from Thomas school buses, that provided the lion's share of passenger service on the G&Q. (Even more fetching were some older German-built Henschel railcars.) The passage through Milagro, a bustling little city, was something special. The railroad ran right down the center of the main street—on the G&Q , a practice more standard than startling—and countless vendors had laid out their wares on the cobbled center island containing the tracks; the whistle announcing our arrival sent them scurrying, parting like water off the bow of a ship, though with a sur-prisingly casual unconcern.

Outside of town we passed a clay pit, with rows and rows of hand-shaped bricks drying in the sun, then headed off through fields of pineapple, sugar cane, and tobacco, as well as vast banana groves. Humble domestic scenes

Baldwin-built Moguls, such as this one, No. 11, crossing the
Rio Yaguachi, were the traditional motive power on the G&Q's
Coastal Division throughout the twentieth century.

opened up one after the other: wash on the line; a woman, barefoot, standing with a broom in a doorway; children framed in glassless windows; pigs
rooting; dogs barking.

By now most of us were perched on the corrugated metal of the baggage-
mail car's gently rounded roof, an uncomfortable but irresistible perch with
360-degree visibility that brought the passing landscape into unparalleled
proximity as we loped along at barely more than a walking pace. Though we
still saw tangent as we looked ahead past the Mogul's shapely domes and tall
stack, the bark of exhaust had quickened and grown steady. Bucay is 975 feet
above sea level, and No. 11 would keep the bit in her teeth the rest of the way
to get there. We stormed into town like conquering heroes as chickens scur-
ried across the tracks and dogs yapped at our heels.

Bucay was a G&Q division point, and rarely has the sense of division been
any more dramatic. The demarcation was between relatively easy railroading
on the *Costa,* stomping ground of the elegant Moguls, to the backbreaking
grades of the *Division Montana,* where even the substantially more power-

The Duran-bound workers' train from Milagro runs through the main street
of Yaguachi. *Autoferros* like this one were common on the G&Q. (ABOVE)

On market day in Bucay, the mixed train is loaded
and ready to depart for Duran. (FACING PAGE)

ful outside-frame 2-8-0's were limited to about 100 tons, which translates
to five cars or fewer. Bucay is something of a cultural division point as well,
between the tropical life of the coastal plain and upland, Indian culture of
the Andes.

Two days earlier, on Sunday (which, like Thursday, was market day), we'd
visited Bucay by minibus to watch the midday arrival of the daily mixtos
between Duran and Alausi, which typically met there to trade locomotives
before continuing on to their destinations. That day the street life had been
dense, and the modest, curving thoroughfare teemed with the buyers and
sellers—of fish, fruits, vegetables, and assorted goods—who had converged
on this little market town. One elderly woman led a pig on a leash. A donkey,
laden with huge bunches of bananas, was tied to a pile of spare rail. The mixed
trains bristled with humanity, crowding flatcars, plus boxcar roofs and in-
sides. Live, tethered chickens, heads darting, waited to board with their new
owners. An old man who had spent his morning with a bottle lurched and
stumbled uncomfortably near the path of a shunting 2-8-0; his grim, fedora-
topped, rifle-toting wife dragged him unceremoniously out of harm's way.

Passenger equipment on the *mixtos* was eclectic, to say the least. There
were handsome, turn-of-the-last-century-style clerestory coaches, home-built

in the Duran shops as recently as the 1970s, some of the newest with plywood sides scribed to look like traditional planking. There were a few eccentric, buslike "streamlined" cars with fluted sides. Colorful in red, white, and blue dress, they seemed a touchingly pathetic attempt at modernity. There were boxcars and flat cars fitted with benches. From Duran to Bucay, fares were

80 sucres (about 45 cents) to ride on the roof, 120 sucres to ride inside a converted boxcar, and a princely 200 sucres for *primera clase,* when the few first-class cars weren't preempted for special trains such as ours.

Bucay was much quieter when we returned on Tuesday by rail, Alausi-bound. Still mindful of staying ahead of the mixto, we didn't dally in trading No. 11 for outside-frame Consolidation No. 45 (Baldwin, 1944), just as red as the Mogul and newly tricked out for our delectation with yellow on handrails, counterweights, domes, and the like. Before long we marched out of town, right down the middle of the curving main street and across the Rio Chimbo; soon afterward we crossed the Rio Chanchan, which we would follow for the next 27 miles, to Sibambe. As we moved through the river's lush semitropical canyon, both the rushing whitewater and sharp, steady stack music told the same story: steepness. For the rest of the day grades ranging from 3 to 5.6 percent would be the norm; in the 35 miles from Bucay to Alausi, we would climb some 6,725 feet.

At Ventura we met the downbound *mixto,* which shuffled into sight behind No. 44, identical sister to our 2-8-0 but painted black instead of red. By now we were all topside, some riding the convenient expanse of the tender's broad oil bunker, others forward on the baggage-mail's roof. We watched the *machinista*—who worked standing up, surefooted in the lurching cab—as if he were an artist. He hauled back on the throttle with his right hand, his left grabbing the loop of the whistle cord to send spine-tingling sounds echoing through the canyon. Butterflies, some yellow, others iridescent blue, floated by our rooftop perch. Along this stretch of the Rio Chanchan we saw the scars of raw earth and new revetments built to deflect raging floodwaters like those of the 1983 El Niño storms that had washed out this section of the railroad. Its reopening in 1988 ended five years of dormancy for the astonishing line we were about to travel.

Mountain-girt Huigra, our next water stop, is something of a Shangri-la. Long known for its healthy climate, it was chosen by Archer Harmon for the G&Q's operating headquarters and staff residences. Today it's a relatively trim, bright little village with a handsome station, a statue of President Eloy Alfaro, and a railroad for a main street, with houses tight on both sides and a precipitous 5 percent grade out of town

Continuing on, we peered ahead for the first glimpse of Nariz del Diablo, the Devil's Nose. This massive granite face harbors the G&Q's greatest engineering ploy, a double switchback with 5.6 percent grades, locally called the Zig-Zag. Riding in the Consolidation's cab, fellow passenger Jeff Stebbins spotted it first, waving and pointing and touching his nose. Then we all saw it: a massive green and gray cone splashed with late afternoon sun, looming directly in our path.

Taking water at Huigra, originally the G&Q's operating headquarters.

There are three short tunnels on this stretch of serpentine railroad along the Chanchan, and riding the roof through them was something of an adventure. We lay flat against the corrugated metal and tried not to breathe, since the tunnels filled with acrid oil smoke from the steadily laboring 2-8-0. And then came another adventure. I was sitting atop the forward end of the baggage car, legs dangling, watching some of our group rocking and rolling on the tender's deck, which on this rough track heaved like a ship in heavy seas. With a sudden explosion of air, the Consolidation became unencumbered of its train and shot ahead, leaving us to travel on our own. Rich Thom, being a veteran Latin American rail rider (and thus no doubt unfazed by such a contretemps), grabbed the brake wheel and brought us to a stop, ending the briefly titillating proposition of a gravity-powered return to Bucay.

Sibambe, located where the Rios Alausi and Guasantos flow together to form the Chanchan, nestles right at the foot of soaring Devil's Nose and was the junction for a rail line running south to Cuenca, Ecuador's third largest city. A handsome station stood in the notch of the junction; from there the main line followed the Rio Alausi up the folds of a canyon to the first switchback. At Sibambe we were caught and passed by the *mixto*, Alco No. 167 in charge of three boxcar loads of riders, but not before it and our train posed for our cameras on the switchbacks.

The trip up the Zig-Zag was riveting for the passengers, routine for the crew. Backing along the second leg, we seemed to be hurtling headlong

Roof-riding on the G&Q.

around blind curves as the engineer nonchalantly hauled back on the throttle and the little Baldwin boiled oil smoke. Directly beneath us, startlingly far away, we could see the roof of the Sibambe station. We spotted the rails we'd just ridden along the Chanchan and others climbing toward Cuenca. After the second switch the grade moderated to 3 percent, then stiffened again as we approached the final challenge: the Alausi Loops, twin horseshoe curves where the ruling grade, 5.6 percent, again applied. As the valley darkened with evening, and only the mountaintops were touched with the last pale sun, roof-riders wished for sweaters.

We arrived at Alausi in a crescendo of sound and expectation, pounding up the middle of the curving main street on a grade that wouldn't quit, whistle howling, exhaust slamming off stucco storefronts. Although we were still moving smartly, little boys ran alongside the tender, grabbing handrails and keeping pace until finally they had the momentum to swing aboard and ride triumphantly the rest of the way through town to the station.

Tucked high up in the Andes, Alausi was another world; not surprisingly, it has long been a rainy-season retreat for Guayaquil residents of means. Virtually carless, the streets were surpassingly peaceful. As we walked up the broad avenue to the Hotel Pan Americano in the chilly dusk, guitar music and singing floated from open windows. A cluster of schoolgirls, neatly dressed

Negotiating the switchbacks on the Devil's Nose.

in white blouses and blue skirts, giggled and skipped arm-in-arm down a side street. A clean, well-lighted place, I thought, remembering Hemingway, high, dry, cool, and welcoming. It was the antithesis of steamy Guayaquil—where, remarkably, we had set out early that same morning.

In Alausi as in Huigra, the backbreaking grade marches right up the main street and through town, on toward the division point of Riobamba and eventually the line's end at Quito. Since the 1983 floods, however, no train had left Alausi for the north, since just outside of town landslides carried away whole hillsides, totally obliterating the right-of-way. The G&Q had been, in effect, two separate railroads for years. Line repair had proceeded by fits and starts since the floods. First the Chanchan washouts were repaired, bringing steam and through trains back to the Zig-Zag and Loops. Eventually line restoration was completed south to Tixan, about 5 miles north of Alausi, and the missing link between those two towns was rough-graded. However, subsequent engineering studies showed the grading to be unsound; the underlying rock was deemed unstable, and the fills were too soft to hold a train. When I traveled, rails had not been laid, though making the railroad whole again was part of a major improvement plan, financed by transportation aid funds provided by French president François Mitterand, that eventually succeeded and would include the arrival of French-built Alstom B-B-B diesels—2,400-horsepower units, akin to some built earlier for Ecuador's 233-mile Ferrocarril Quito & San Lorenzo (completed in 1957 to provide a shorter link to the coast than the G&Q).

After a day moseying around Alausi, the Loops, and the Zig-Zag with our Consolidation-powered charter train, we set out for Cuenca aboard autoferro No. 97, Thomas-built, in Quito. This was a no-frills vehicle. The sander, for instance, was a tin cup, a bucket of sand, and a hole in the floor to pour it through. But the windshield was festooned with brightly colored tassels. We careened down the Loops and Zig-Zag like a Lionel train in the hands of an exuberant child, then switched off onto the 89-mile-long Ferrocarril Sibambe & Cuenca, begun in 1915 and not completed until 1965. Though originally autonomous, the S&C, along with the G&Q and the Ferrocarril Quito & San Lorenzo, became part of the State Railways of Ecuador: Empresa Nacional de Ferrocarriles del Estado, or ENFE, created in 1970.

Right-of-way decrepitude had kept the S&C strictly an autoferro operation since washouts damaged the line in 1981. From the rooftop luggage rack, I watched as the S&C line scaled the valley wall until the Rio Chanchan and the G&Q to Bucay were far below. All around was the green of mountains, soft, folded velvet dappled with cloud shadows. On one sharp horseshoe curve, a cluster of white crosses at trackside marked the spot of a particularly grisly derailment. After a lunch stop we rattled on to Azogues, 17 miles from Cuenca. A "tourist train"—actually patronized mostly by school groups, from what we could see—had just begun operating between those two cities with Mogul No. 14, an exact sister to No. 11 and similarly modernized. We ran into Cuenca just ahead of the excursion train.

The next day, by bus, we journeyed to Tixan (with a stop to tour the Incan ruins at Ingapirca), where we boarded our final charter train for a 194-mile, two-day journey to Quito, with an overnight stop at Riobamba. Hauled by Alco diesel No. 164, our train began as one boxcar plus a single coach, not *primera clase,* as apparently none were available at this end of the line. The hard, backless bench seats that ran the length of the car were not especially comfortable, and the Alco's fumes, coupled with the higher speeds on this relatively level line, kept us inside.

Though an anticlimax, this journey across the sierra was not without its memorable moments. After all, this inter-Andean route is called the "Avenue of Volcanoes," with good reason: some 22 of them line the railroad. At Palmira, where we stopped for a photo runby, we scuffed through the volcanic ash that covered the ground. From Tixan to Quito, elevations would vary from 9,000 to nearly 11,000 feet, with Quito itself being 9,375 feet above sea level.

Dusk darkened into night as we neared Riobamba. Inside our coach, the brakeman unpacked and lit his kerosene lantern, which glowed cozily in the deepening blue-gray. It flickered on the faces of tired travelers who lurched and swayed toward a comfortable room and ample dinner at Hosteria Andaluza, a 400-year-old hacienda-turned-hotel, located 10 miles from Riobamba and nestled at the base of 20,689-foot Chimborazo, the highest of the volcanoes.

At Riobamba, bordered by flower gardens, S&C Consolidation No. 15 stood on display, masquerading with G&Q tender lettering. This was the only steam locomotive on the Quito end of the line, which has been dieselized for two decades and was now operated by a pair of Alco-Eskaldunas and autoferros, which provided Riobamba-Quito service daily except Sundays. Some years earlier, Espreso Metropolitan Touring had refit a coach with a large retractable observation platform, parlor seats, galley, and bar, originally for use between Guayaquil and Riobamba via the Devil's Nose; since the floods severed the line, this car had offered Quito-Riobamba tours coupled to the end of the mixto.

Riobamba was once the site of the G&Q's main locomotive shops, and its substantial stub-end terminal spoke of former importance. At misty, desolate Urbina, 20 miles further on, elevation 11,841 feet, we reached the highest point on the railroad, marked by a handsome old stucco station trying bravely to be contemporary in white dress with bands of blue and red paint. Low clouds dropped light rain on this empty, end-of-the-world spot, where I stood on the cobblestones of the old Pan American Highway to photograph our little train. A few Indians crossed the tracks, dressed in the inevitable fedoras and ponchos and headed for who knows where in that desolate void.

This marked the second of three ranges of the Andes that our special would cross. The first had come the previous afternoon, at Palmira, 10,628 feet; the third, at Cotopaxi (11,638 feet), was some four hours ahead. Virtually all day we passed volcanoes, beginning with Chimborazo, Carlhuairazo, Altar, and Tunguraha, all snowcapped, all visible from Riobamba. Headed into Cotopaxi we were overtaken by the Riobamba-Quito Autoferro, which ran right on our heels, close enough for us to read the driver's lips, until Cotopaxi, where it jockeyed past us and headed for home: Quito.

That evening we arrived there, too—rail-weary, feeling something like pioneers to have accomplished all but the obliterated few of the 281 rugged miles from Guayaquil, built with so much difficulty between 1871 and 1908. Along the way we'd passed through a land where ancient Baldwins had risen from the fires of dieselization and flooded rail beds for a final, fantastic flight.

A Silverton-bound train pounds upgrade along the Animas River. (ABOVE)

The conductor and attendant wait to board *Cinco Animas* passengers prior to departure from Silverton. (BELOW)

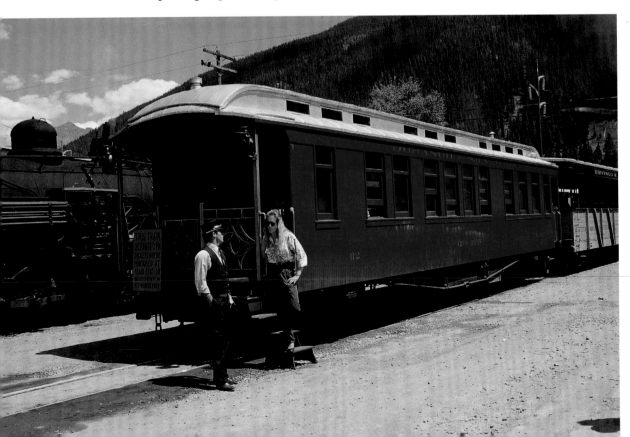

8

THE SILVERTON

FRAMED IN THE TALL REAR WINDOWS OF THE *CINCO ANIMAS*, a diminutive wooden business car of venerable heritage, Colorado's San Juan Mountains soared skyward. Narrow-gauge rails spun off behind, weaving back and forth to follow the tumbling waters of the Animas River— the Rio de las Animas Perdidas, or River of the Lost Souls. With our small group of family and friends—Laurel, Jennifer and Emily, Rich and Linda Thom, and me—comfortably ensconced in this historic car, the train rattled and rolled downgrade through a bright August afternoon, heading back to Durango at a leisurely pace from the picture-book, false-fronted Victorian mining town of Silverton, a National Historic Landmark with a fine collection of period buildings.

The fragrance of coal smoke drifted back from the 480, a chunky K-36 outside-frame Mikado built in 1925 by Baldwin Locomotive Works. The oak and birch paneling aboard the *Cinco Animas* creaked, and wheels on rail sang. Now and again No. 480's engineer laid on the whistle cord, and a melodious warning echoed off canyon walls. Riding the *Cinco Animas*, we enjoyed the rail-bound perquisites of privacy and comfort once reserved for nabobs and railroad presidents—who, in fact, had been among the *Cinco's* passengers in the car's earlier days. But in 1991, when we rode the *Cinco Animas,* the Durango & Silverton Narrow Gauge Railroad routinely offered that car—and the *Nomad,* an even more opulent former business car (and, in fact, the car we'd originally chosen)—to anyone, on a charter basis, for a price.

For the entire 45-mile journey on the Durango & Silverton, probably the most famous steam railway in the United States, our train—yellow coaches, open cars, and, on the end, the *Cinco Animas,* gleaming in distinctive red livery—rarely strayed from the river. In its upper reaches, where the tracks ran directly alongside, the water danced and sparkled in the sunlight; farther downstream the Animas plunged precipitously, leaving the rail line high above to slink along a narrow ledge hacked out of vertical cliff. Here the river swirled in deep, narrow flows. As the locomotive tiptoed along the "High Line," those of us peering from the open observation platform into the abyss plunging sheer just a few feet from the tracks admitted that a jolt of adrenalin underscored our appreciation of nature's majesty.

From Silverton down to Rockwood, a distance of 27 miles, the railroad ran through wilderness, and since there were no roads, the train was the way in and out for hikers and fishermen. At Elk Park, deep in the two million acre San Juan National Park, the K-36 eased to a stop, panting softly. As passengers leaned out of coach windows to watch, hikers slung their backpacks down from the boxcar at the head of the train, then hopped off themselves. We watched as they shouldered their packs. Then the locomotive whistled off, headed once again toward Durango, leisurely stack talk echoing softly off the mountains, the time-honored steam engine symphony. The hikers waved to the departing train, then did a double take as the red-liveried luxury of the *Cinco Animas* rolled by.

By turns we stood on the open observation platform to watch the nonstop scenery receding in our wake, or sat inside—either in the somewhat Spartan, inward-facing straight-backed chairs in the rearmost lounge or in the plush red seats of the cozier central area of the car. This atmospheric room still contained four Pullman sections: wide seats that could be made down into lower berths at night, while uppers folded from the ceiling.

Both the Durango & Silverton and the cars now known as *Cinco Animas* and *Nomad* are rich in accumulated lore. As much as the scenery, this genuine historicity is responsible for the line's uniqueness—and for its being named a National Historic Landmark in 1967 and National Historic Civil Engineering Landmark the next year. The D&S, and the Cumbres & Toltec Scenic Railroad, some 100 miles from Durango, are remnants of a once-vast spider web of 3-foot-gauge rails that crisscrossed Colorado. In 1882, when the Denver & Rio Grande completed its Silverton Branch from Durango, the final piece of the San Juan Extension from Alamosa via Chama, the system was approaching its zenith: more than 1,800 route miles in a network that reached from

In August 1969, this Silverton Branch work train headed
out of Durango created an inadvertently historic image.

Denver as far west as Salt Lake City and Ogden, Utah, and as far south as
Santa Fe, New Mexico.

Largely a product of the gold and silver mining boom, the D&RG chose
narrow gauge because it was less costly to build in the mountainous terrain
that characterizes Colorado, particularly important in boom times, which all
too soon could turn to bust. Turn they did, and through the middle decades
of the last century the far-flung Rio Grande narrow gauge was systematically
standard-gauged or, more frequently, abandoned. Silverton-Branch passenger
service, however, quietly evolved from a coach and caboose running behind
freight cars in a twice-weekly mixed train to a daily (in summer) string of
yellow coaches carrying tourists. From a low of fewer than 2,000 passengers
annually, ridership grew to over 50,000.

Both the yellow color (replacing traditional green) and perhaps some of
the popularity resulted from the Silverton train's appearance in numerous
movies, from *Ticket to Tomahawk, Denver & Rio Grande* (for which the railroad sacrificed a pair of 2-8-0's to a head-end collision, assuming that they

would never be wanted in the future), and *Around the World in 80 Days* to *Butch Cassidy and the Sundance Kid*. As the 1960s dawned, the Denver & Rio Grande Western was embarrassed by the little remnant of narrow gauge—the San Juan Extension, plus a branch south from Durango to Farmington, New Mexico—that it was forced to operate and particularly embarrassed by the aged steam locomotives that plied it. In 1962 the railroad tried to abandon the Silverton Branch, but its request was emphatically denied by the Interstate Commerce Commission, which pointed out that the line was returning a robust profit.

Making a virtue of necessity, the D&RGW took a different course and worked to maximize returns. This led to the "Rio Grande Land" project, which involved the purchase for development of two blocks on Main Street in Durango near the depot. In 1963 and 1964, to increase passenger capacity on the train, the railroad built eight new all-steel cars at its Burnham Shops in Denver; with their scribed steel sides, they were nearly identical in external appearance to the old wooden cars still in service. In addition, also at Burnham, three roofed open cars were constructed from drop-end pipe gondolas—themselves rebuilt, in 1953, from standard-gauge boxcars. This allowed the Rio Grande to add a second train. In 1967 came three more open cars.

However, the real growth, and it was dramatic, occurred in 1981 when the railroad sold the branch to Florida citrus magnate Charles Bradshaw for a reported $2.2 million. He renamed it the Durango & Silverton Narrow Gauge Railroad and brought about welcome changes that the D&RGW had chosen not to make or claimed were impossible.

First addressed was the matter of the fake diamond stacks worn since 1956 by the trio of K-28 Mikados that for decades had been the line's only locomotives. These ungainly, inauthentic smokestacks were introduced to backdate one of the locomotives, actually built in 1923, for a role in a movie. Tourism had already become the lifeblood of the Silverton Branch, so the top-heavy, inappropriate diamond stacks, thought to make the train more atmospheric, found favor with the Rio Grande, and all three K-28 survivors (from 10 originally built) came to wear them. One of Bradshaw's first directives was their removal, revealing the tall shotgun stacks (which had lurked there, hidden, all along) that had originally been characteristic of the lines of the locomotives, which the crews had dubbed "sport models." But the changes Bradshaw wrought were far more than simply cosmetic.

"We're running a railroad, not an amusement park ride," he said, and this meant moving people or things, as many and as much as possible, whenever and wherever there was demand. Whatever freight was available the railroad hauled willingly. After years of absence, yellow "express" boxcars headed consists to carry gear for backpackers, who were welcomed to ride to trail-

In 1960, the Durango roundhouse is alive overnight with power for the Silverton train—a K-28 still carrying a bogus diamond stack—and heavier locomotives for freights to Farmington and Chama.

heads deep in the Animas River canyon. (Back in 1971, when I had ridden into the canyon to fish Elk Creek, a tributary of the Animas, the railroad had been doing nothing to promote this option, although they were required by charter to provide it.)

The imperative to haul more passengers led to a huge innovation in the D&SNGRR's first year: the improvement of track, bridges, and clearances on the branch to allow operation of the larger, fat-boiled K-36 and K-37 Mikados and the refurbishment of K-36 No. 481, numerical neighbor of the K-36 that would be our power when we rode the *Cinco Animas*. The K-36's had been built by Baldwin in 1925; the slightly heavier K-37's, numbered in the 490's, were rebuilds from 1902 Baldwin Consolidations, done in Burnham Shops in 1928 and 1930. Six of these heftier locomotives—the two K-36's and four K-37's—were included in Bradshaw's purchase of the Silverton Branch.

An engineering survey had identified the work required to prepare the line to receive this new breed of Silverton engine: widening Rockwood Cut and increasing clearances elsewhere, particularly on the High Line, improving certain stretches of the roadbed, and strengthening some bridges and trestles. All this—which for years the Rio Grande had insisted was impractical—was accomplished in short order. This allowed longer trains, since the larger 2-8-2's were more powerful, and more trains, as more of the larger locomotives were rebuilt. In addition the season was expanded—even into winter, with the operation of a short turn from Durango as far as Cascade Canyon, a bit more than halfway to Silverton.

In the decade between the Bradshaw purchase and our private-car journey, the D&S had rebuilt enough additional locomotives and cars to allow the operation of an astonishing five daily round-trips in peak season—four covering the whole line, with an additional departure from Durango (the last of the day) turning at Cascade Canyon. In 1991 the D&S carried over 200,000 riders annually, a hundredfold increase over patronage at the nadir.

Our ride aboard the *Cinco* was far from my first experience with the Silverton Train. In time the Colorado narrow gauge became my grand passion in railroading, which I deemed fully worthy of the many books written about it and the many visits I'd make there. To begin at the beginning—the beginning for me, which is much earlier than any other experience chronicled in this volume—takes the story back to August 1960. I was 16. Roger Cook, my friend and neighbor, was a crucial year or so older than I, meaning that he had a New Jersey driver's license. He was not, however, old enough to rent a car, which makes this story glancingly about my father.

I was in Salt Lake City with my parents, visiting my grandmother, cousins, and the rest of my mother's large family there. In an act of faith and generosity that I dearly hope I appreciated at the time, Dad flew with me—aboard a Frontier Airlines DC-3—to Grand Junction, Colorado, to rent a car for us, then flew back to Salt Lake, making possible our brief foray into the wonderland of narrow-gauge steam. Before following a freight to Farmington, and the next day a double-header to Chama, we devoted a day to riding the Silverton train—in retrospect a mistake, since that experience would be equally available half a century later.

This was the Silverton of the touristic but unexpanded format: two gondolas filled with ties, a baggage car and combine with concession stand, and coaches, all original, all wooden. The journey had the exhilaration of newness, no doubt partly because I spent much of it at the window of the forward-facing door of the baggage car talking with Gervaise, a redheaded girl from Lake Charles, Louisiana, who was about my chronological age but older otherwise. This fed a growing interest of mine that for a time would push railroading to the back burner.

At Needleton tank in 1960, a K-28 has its tender refreshed with enough water to finish the run into Silverton. The ties in the two gondolas will help maintain the branch, which was growing in tourist ridership.

On a February afternoon in 2008, K-27 No. 478 tiptoes
out on the High Line, running toward Cascade Canyon.

Of the Durango & Silverton's mixed bag of old, new, and repurposed rolling stock, no cars are more interesting than the *Cinco Animas* and the *Nomad;*
like the railroad itself, they're lucky to be around. Both cars have convoluted
histories that include disasters, near-disasters, and multiple rebuildings. Depending on how you look at it, you could say that the *Cinco Animas* was built
in 1879 as a Horton Chair Car with swivel seats (what we would call a parlor
car) and soon converted to a pay car, which traveled the railroad dispensing
wages to employees. But in another rebuilding (following a major wreck in
1909), its identity was muddled when the car traded bodies with a similar
wooden coach (built in 1883) that happened to be in the railroad's Burnham
Shops at the same time. The *Cinco Animas* as it exists today is recognizably a
product of yet *another* rebuilding, this one in 1917, when the car became the
B-2 (*B* for "business car"), part of a luxurious official train. It was fitted with
a master bedroom (which has since become the kitchen), along with a rear
parlor and, in the middle of the car, four sections. These latter two areas are
still intact, with original paneling.

The B-2 was badly damaged in a shop fire in 1953 and subsequently sold
to an Oklahoma City railfan, who placed it in his backyard. A decade later
the car was purchased and brought back home by five Durango-area busi-
nessmen, acting as the Cinco Animas Corporation: the "Five Souls," with
a nod to the local Animas River. The Five Souls turned one vestibule of the
B-2 into an open observation platform, painted the car red, and dubbed it the

Cinco Animas. From 1964 onward—after more than eight decades of wreck, fire, rebuildings, reassignments, confused identities, and dislocation—the car finally achieved stability, remaining available for service on the Silverton train.

The *Nomad,* the D&S's other private car available for charter, was at least as illustrious and luxurious as the *Cinco Animas,* and its career was hardly less convoluted. It began life in 1878, also as a Horton Chair Car, but less than a decade later was reconfigured as a business car, part of an "Executive Office Train." Rebuilt and redesignated a number of times, the car in 1909 hosted President William Howard Taft—a big man in a little car.

Badly damaged in a wreck on the Silverton Branch in 1917, the car emerged from the shops looking basically as it does today: open observation platform with ornate railing, fold-down Pullman-type berths at its forward end, a master bedroom in the middle, a large parlor at the rear, and birch and mahogany paneling throughout. The car entered private ownership is 1951. By 1982, when the D&S bought the *Nomad* (as it was named in 1957), it had changed hands five times (the Cinco Animas Corporation owned it, too, for many years) and had had its interior thoroughly renovated to a Victorian appearance. Wearing its traditional dark-green livery, the car today retains an opulent feel, with a brass bed in the stateroom, heavily cushioned chairs and sofa in the rear lounge, and fringed velvet curtains throughout.

Both these business cars have had their harrowing moments, and the *Nomad* stubbed its toe again on August 3, 1991, when—apparently due to a brakeman's error in prematurely throwing a switch—the stately business car derailed at low speed and rolled over on its side, remaining out of service for the better part of a month, the reason our charter plans had to be changed. But we were happy aboard the *Cinco Animas* and sorry when our journey had to end, which it did as the Mikado chugged easily through broad meadows, with the red Hermosa Cliffs off to the east—a gentle letdown after the spectacle of the canyon. Then we loped into Durango, passing the quintessentially Victorian Strater Hotel and stopping at the depot, places already replete with memories for Laurel and me.

Over the years we'd bellied up to the bar in the hotel's Diamond Belle Saloon, listening to rinky-tink tunes pounded out on an old upright piano. We'd stayed in the hotel's thrifty, basic accommodations designated "sleeping rooms," good for little else, and once luxuriously in one of the top-rated rooms with a bay window from which we could watch the trains en route to Silverton. From the depot, we'd wandered unchallenged into the nearby roundhouse on more than one placid evening to soak in the sights, sounds, and smells of steam locomotives at rest.

Now, after riding a Denver & Rio Grande business car, we'd added another memory.

Steam-powered trains meet in the bright morning sun at Wernigerode-Westerntor, the headquarters of the HSB. (ABOVE)

In Wernigerode, children on their way to school
wait for the train to pass. (BELOW)

9

STEAMING THROUGH
THE HARZ MOUNTAINS

WHEN THE IRON CURTAIN FELL, COMMUNIST BLOC countries suddenly lay open to the Stateside traveler much like a late winter landscape revealed by melting snow. Predictably, many of the uncovered vistas were dispiriting, drab, littered landscapes of despair. But amid the gray detritus were some glittering gems, like the Harzer Schmalspurbahnen—the Harz Mountain Narrow Gauge Railways, or HSB, in former East Germany—and Wernigerode, the ancient city that is their operating headquarters.

I arrived at the Schmalspurbahnen's Wernigerode station, adjacent to the platforms of the Deutsche Bahn, Germany's now-unified national rail system, on a warm September afternoon in 1994. Waiting there was a string of diminutive red-and-cream coaches lettered "HSB"; at the head end, a shiny black locomotive, a 2-10-2T, steamed quietly, with fragrant coal smoke curling from its stack. Wheels, driving rods, and frame were neatly tricked out in red. I boarded the third coach; soon, with a shrill and urgent whistle cry, the husky little locomotive lurched into motion. We were bound at a stately pace for Brocken, 2,900 feet higher up in the Harz Mountains and minutely visible dead ahead of the chuffing locomotive. We threaded our way among

startlingly picturesque half-timber, tile-roofed shops and houses that fronted winding streets, then paused briefly at Wernigerode-Westerntor, where a
handsome stucco depot presided over platforms dotted with flower boxes.
Adjacent stood the railroad's sprawling shop buildings, industrial architecture in classic brick. The coach I was riding had been made there.

Once into the mountains, our engine began to talk it up, its exhaust steady
and loud to announce a climb that would continue virtually unrelieved all
the way to Brocken. The HSB's tracks are meter gauge. However, the locomotive—from a fleet of 17 built between 1954 and 1956 that were the HSB's
everyday engines—was more bruiser than ballerina, with a hulking boiler
atop 10 driving wheels, small for good traction. These are tank engines, no
tenders, with water carried in tanks astride the boiler and coal in a bunker
at the rear. However, these chunky, hefty, no-nonsense brawlers bear little
resemblance to Thomas, the smiling, anthropomorphic little tank engine created by Reverend W. D. Awdry. Older locomotives on the Harz roster—eight
all told, including a quartet of 0-4-4-0T Mallets, articulated compounds,
three of which had been built in 1897 and 1898 for the Nordhausen-Werni-
grode Eisenbahn—did appear on occasion, though, and they were more like
Thomas and his pals Oliver and Percy.

The HSB had three parts when I visited, all operated as a single railroad.
The Harzquerbahn ran 38 miles north-south from Wernigerode to Nordhausen Nord. At Drei Annen Hohne, 12 miles from Wernigerode, the Brockenbahn, my route for the first day of my visit, veered off. These two lines had
been built in 1896 as the Nordhausen-Wernigerode Eisenbahn (or railway,
literally "iron road"). At Eisfelder Talmuhle, 18 miles further on, the Selket-
albahn forks eastward, extending 32 miles to Gernrode, with additional
branches to Hasselfelde and Harzgerode. Originally this was all part of the
Gernrode-Harzgerode Eisenbahn, built a decade earlier than the NWE, in
1886. (A third line, the Süd Harz Eisenbahn, finished in 1897, had been cut off
from the balance of the system by the post–World War II East-West German
border and was lifted in 1963.)

These distances are short, but the steep grades, sharp curves, and
leisurely stops to meet other trains and take on water conspired to make
them seem far longer. At Drei Annen Hohne, for instance, while our Brock-
en-bound train loaded passengers, the fireman swung the spout in place
to top off our tanks. Meanwhile, a whistle around the bend announced
a Nordhausen-Wernigerode train that rambled into the station on a passing
track.

As we swung onto the Brocken branch we entered national park land.
Schierke, a few miles further on, was as far as the highway went, so the remaining empty seats on the train filled. The clientele was decidedly middle-aged
to elderly, but vigorous, outdoor types. The coaches—clean and perfectly

A crew member fills a thirsty 2-10-2T's side tanks with water.

comfortable, if spartan—had one great feature: windows that opened far enough for me to squeeze my head out and watch the locomotive churn and flail along, hoisted up the mountain on an alternating succession of curves. Here and there the deep evergreen forest broke away, and then the vistas were far and fine.

Approaching the summit, the train wrapped around the mountain in a tightening spiral. As we popped into the open, above timberline, the exhaust barked louder, as if the engine were giving its last ounce of energy for the final climb. Here a trail paralleled the tracks; hikers, many with walking sticks, exchanged waves with train passengers. Some snapped pictures of the train as we passed. Then suddenly the clamor ceased and we were there, on a bald summit that seemed the top of the world. The trip, 21 strenuous miles all told, had taken an hour and 40 minutes. Peering from my coach window, I could see the orange-tile roofs of Wernigerode, a toy village far below.

In *Faust,* Goethe (who visited Wernigerode in 1777) set his witches' sabbath in the Harz Mountains, and Brocken did have an otherworldly, almost sinister quality—a barren landscape with whistling wind and scudding clouds. But the most ominous presence was a vast Sputnik-like tower and antenna that bristled skyward. The highest summit in the Harz Mountains, Brocken is in a part of former East Germany that bulged into the West. These two characteristics made it perfect for a top-secret Soviet listening post and radar location, which is what all the fancy electronics were about. As a result, Brocken was off limits and the line was closed to passengers from 1961 to 1992. Judging by the crowds when I rode, people were glad to be able to go hiking at Brocken again. A significant number of passengers who had ridden upgrade disembarked and hiked down, but not me.

However, my lazy ride downhill, with the engine running tank-first, was an anticlimax. Brake shoes squealed to hold back the train on the steep grades. I dozed. But I woke up fast enough when, back in Wernigerode, I discovered the *Marktplatz,* where I was staying at the Hotel Weisser Hirsch, "the White Deer." Stepping into this cobbled square literally brought me up short, as if I'd been thrust into a movie set, only this was real.

Across from the hotel was the *Rathaus,* or town hall—an exquisite gingerbread pile of towers, turrets, bays, and cupola that, in its current form,

Digging into the stiff grade to Brocken.

dates from 1544. The *Marktplatz* was bounded by curving streets that spun off in various directions. Classic half-timbered architecture, most from the sixteenth and seventeenth centuries, was everywhere. Luminous in late afternoon, with last sun splashing ornate storefronts, the scene was a perfection of brick, stucco, wood, and stone in a lively palette of colors.

Amid flowerboxes spilling blooms, I sat at a table in front of the hotel, ordered a half-liter of the local beer—Hasseroder Pils, beautifully rich and bracingly bitter—and watched night fall. The peace was pervasive. An ornate metal fountain spouted discreetly in mid-square, and every 15 minutes the Rathaus clock chimed. Puffy clouds turned pink. Townspeople, mostly couples, wandered across the square. Bicycles buzzed by, but no cars.

When it got chilly I repaired to the hotel's cheerful, cozy dining room. From a hefty, leather-bound, multipage menu I selected sauerbraten, potato dumplings, and red cabbage—one of my favorite meals, further recommended by the fact that it was among the few items I could read on the German menu. Though the Harz Mountains region has long catered to tourists, and though I felt hospitably welcomed everywhere, no one I met—at the hotel, on the railroad, or elsewhere—spoke more than a few words of English, and most spoke none. In that respect Wernigerode was typical of towns once behind the Iron Curtain and hugely different from West Germany.

The history of the little railroads in the Harz Mountains reflects the region's broader history. Built in the late nineteenth century—in meter gauge, to better negotiate the tight curves and steep grades mandated by the mountains—this network of private lines primarily served the mining and timber industries. Like so many others, these railways benefited from the dramatic growth of tourism in the early twentieth century, then suffered from the ascendancy of the automobile in the 1930s. After World War II, in 1946, one of the original lines, the Gernrode-Harzgeroder Eisenbahn, was actually largely dismantled and carried away by the Soviet Union as war reparations. Almost immediately, the Soviets recognized this as an error, and by 1949 much of it was rebuilt and open to traffic. The last section was not restored until 1983, however.

In 1949, Deutsche Reichsbahn (East Germany's nationalized railway, incorporated along with West Germany's Deutsche Bundesbahn into Deutsche Bahn after German reunification in 1990) took over operation of the system. Though the Brocken line was closed to the public, the planned-economy days of Communism were generally good ones for the Harz railways, as private automobile ownership was limited. Small operating losses were routinely subsidized. On the other hand, limited resources were available for upgrading, which meant the survival of steam. As has so often been the case, benign neglect and lack of funds for modernization proved preservation's best allies. In 1974 the Harz lines were designated a national monument.

With the German reunification, things had changed. Freight traffic had fallen to nothing, and automobiles were proliferating. In February 1993, the little trains were privatized (something of a misnomer, since state and local governments were the new owners) as the Harzer Schmalspurbahnen. Since then they'd been expected to earn their keep. The Brockenbahn, I thought, should have had no trouble doing that, but judging from what I saw in my second day of traveling the system, the rest might be far more problematic.

After a fine buffet breakfast at the Weisser Hirsch—rolls, cheeses, jams, cold meats, fruit, and more—I made the short walk to the Wernigerode Westerntor station where, later that morning, I'd start a journey that would include much of the HSB. Two women were busy washing the windows of a string of coaches. From the platform, I watched through the station's bay window as the agent grabbed and cranked a lever, causing the red-and-white crossing gate behind me to drop down, mechanically ratcheting a warning gong as it went. A little girl with a school bag rushed to beat the dropping gate, lost the race, considered the situation for a while, then—since the train was not yet in sight—scooted under. Diesel-powered, this was the 7:12 to Nordhausen Nord.

I wandered down to the engine shed, some distance from the station, and spotted something tantalizing: green-boilered 0-4-4-0T No. 13 steaming quietly in front of the engine house. It was great seeing the locomotive, then only a few years short of its centennial, out in the open. I surmised that it was steamed up for some special train; lacking the language, however, I would never find out, and in any case my inflexible ongoing itinerary called for my leaving just a few short hours from then, so with regret I turned my back on tiny No. 13 and headed back to the station.

My Nordhausen-bound train, the 10:30, I was pleased to see, would be steam-powered. Since the HSB was an independent railroad, not part of Deutsche Bahn, my Eurailpass wasn't valid, so I purchased tickets, *Fahrkartes*, in the station. They were all-purpose forms, with "Wernigerode-Westerntor," the point of purchase, entered with a rubber stamp and departure and arrival stations and fare filled in with pencil: 16 Deutsche marks to Alexisbad, 12 from there to Nordhausen-Nord. (My much shorter ride on the far more popular ride to Brocken had cost 19 marks.) On board, I handed my ticket to the friendly conductor—young, like virtually all I encountered in my two days of riding, and, like many, female

It was déjà vu for me as far as Drei Annen Hohne, retracing the previous day's steps. There we were one of three trains arriving at once, indicative of both the frequency of service and the exemplary timekeeping that allowed such clockwork connections. All told the timetable for that summer listed eight round-trips to Brocken and five between Wernigerode and Nordhausen-Nord. Trains were coming and going in all directions.

One of them was hauled by a hulking red diesel, at that time the fly in the steam-lover's ointment on the HSB. In the late 1980s, for freight service, the railroad bought 10 standard-gauge diesels and stuck them on narrow-gauge trucks, not an aesthetic triumph. After this freight service had dried up, the diesels entered the passenger pool—appearing, during my visit at least, completely at random, which seemed odd to me, considering that the HSB's future appeared to be as a tourist attraction and steam was the draw. Of the 30 trains I saw in two days, a dozen were diesel-hauled.

Beyond Drei Annen Hohne I was covering new ground, and the scenery gradually changed from mountainous to bucolic. Passengers became scarce, and I shared a coach with just an elderly couple and their lap dog. Just outside of Benneckenstein we eased to a stop at a semaphore, and I heard whistling up ahead. Soon the blade clanked to vertical, and we pulled into the station next to the once-a-day Nordhausen-Brocken train, with which we swapped locomotives before being on our way to Eisfelder Talmuhle.

"Umsteigen! Umsteigen!" the conductor said with some urgency when we arrived there, seeing that my ticket was to Alexisbad, but I already knew I had to disembark and change trains. At Eisfelder Talmuhle, in sharp contrast to the bustle at Drei Annen Hohne and Schierke, the platforms were empty. Stucco peeled in chunks from the brick depot. *"Gaststätte ist geschlossen"* read a hand-lettered sign on the locked door of the station restaurant.

While the fireman filled the locomotive's tanks, the couple walked their dog. Then the train whistled off and headed briskly for Nordhausen, leaving me alone with nothing to do but wait for my train to Steige, with a connection to Alexisbad. From here on, one hand was adequate to tally the passengers aboard as we rattled along through pleasantly rolling hills that admittedly lacked the excitement of mountains and steep grades. One memorable moment of drama did remain, however, and it came at 4:24 PM, as I left Alexisbad for the return to Eisfelder Talmuhle and ongoing connection for Nordhausen. Also scheduled out at exactly 4:24 was a train for the branch to Harzgerode.

The two trains marched out of town neck-and-neck, on parallel tracks, we diesel-hauled, the Harzgerode train behind steam. We growled, he barked; we blatted, he hooted, the spine-chilling, unmistakable hoot of the European steam locomotive. Engine crews shouted and waved back and forth until, finally, the branch line fell away from the main line and the other horse in harness disappeared off into the woods, leaving behind a fragrant pall of coal smoke.

View from the forward compartment of the *Crystal Panoramic Express.* (ABOVE)

For passengers not accommodated in the forward compartment, the main lounge is a more than acceptable alternative. (LEFT)

10

NEW TRAINS, OLD BOATS
IN SWITZERLAND

THE FRENCH DOORS OF MY UPPER-FLOOR ROOM AT
Montreux's Hotel Suisse-Majestic framed a slate gray, rain-swept
Lake Geneva, also called Lac Léman. With the September dusk, the water
was darkening, and a chill was in the air. Far down the lake, two clusters of
lights materialized. Slowly, the bright pinpoints became a pair of lanky white
paddle steamers churning toward me in stately fashion, with deck and saloon
lights festively ablaze. The first—*La Suisse,* on a dinner cruise—whistled a
throaty salute as she passed. The second, *Italie,* eased up to the landing below
my perch. Although she had the same graceful, traditional profile as *La Suisse,*
her honking horn gave away her secret: her steam plant had been replaced by
diesel engines.

I had arrived from Lausanne a few hours earlier aboard sister side-
wheeler *Montreux,* built in 1904, the oldest boat in the fleet of eight traditional
steamers. (The newest dates from 1927.) In spite of this antiquity, when I
boarded I felt the unwelcome rumble and growl underfoot that said "diesel."
At that time, in 1994, the fleet of the Compagnie Generale de Navigation
sur le Lac Léman comprised (in addition to some modern diesel vessels)
four steam-powered boats and four converted paddle steamers. (Since then,
mirabile dictu, the *Montreux* has been converted back to steam propulsion.)

Although I'd hoped for a steamboat, I knew I'd soon have the chance to sail aboard steam-powered craft on other lakes.

Meanwhile, I walked along rain-slicked streets to dinner at the Caveau du Museum, a cheery, bustling bistro in the basement of a thirteenth-century monastery, now a museum. Fondue and raclette filled the cozy room with a fromage fragrance. Montreux has a wonderful compactness, wedged between the shore of Lake Geneva and the Vaudois Alps. In addition to having its own attractions, the city is a gateway to great places. For example, I was headed to the summit of the Rothorn, elevation 7,710 feet—an easy one-day trip, although I would use two boats and four trains, two of them narrow-gauge, to get there.

The back door of the Suisse-Majestic was just a block from the boat landing, while the front door was right across from the train station, which serves not only the Swiss Federal Railway's main line from Geneva to Italy via Brig and the Simplon Tunnel but also two narrow-gauge mountain railways: the Chemin de Fer Montreux-Glion-Rochers-de-Nayes, a rack-and-pinion line built in 2-foot 7½-inch gauge, and the meter-gauge mixed rack and adhesion Montreux-Oberland Bernois. The MOB's most important route is its 37-mile line up and over the mountains to Zweisimmen, where it connects with a branch of the standard-gauge Berne Lötschberg Simplon Railway for a 22-mile run to Spiez.

Though the MOB's trains are narrow-gauge, they're anything but old-fashioned. In fact, my train, the *Crystal Panoramic Express,* roughly a year old at the time, had a decidedly space-age sleekness to it. Electric-powered (900 volts D.C. in this case) like most Swiss trains, the *Crystal Panoramic Express* positioned its locomotive in the middle of the train, a most unusual practice, making it literally bidirectional. At both ends were cars with broad, high, wrap-around windshields. With the engineer sequestered in an overhead control cab, the glass-enclosed forward space on the main level was available for two rows of passenger seating—the place to be.

These fore and aft cars also featured stylish bar-lounges with sofas and club chairs, while traditional coach-style seating filled the train's other two cars. All had dome-style skylights for brightness and viewing. But I was happy to have snagged one of the forward seats as the train eased away from Montreux's station and zigzagged up the mountainside behind the city. It was another rainy day, but long, spidery wipers swept the splatters off the windshield.

Now Lake Geneva was on the left, now on the right, now on the left again as tracks hoisted our streamlined blue-and-white train ever higher above water and cityscape. We soon overtook a local that had left Montreux a few minutes ahead of us (an admirable, leisurely ride in its own right, with windows that could be opened to the crisp alpine air). Our express hummed

The paddle steamer *Blümlisalp* provided the link from
Spiez to Interlaken West across Lake Thun.

along, speed unchecked, and in fact made only two station stops on its one
hour, 36-minute run.

This line is one of Switzerland's oldest, completed between 1901 and 1905.
It's long been part of an important through routing linking Zurich with Geneva: the Golden Pass Route. Its preeminence led to MOB's inaugurating
the posh *Golden Mountain Pullman Express* in 1931—an abject failure, as
it turned out, brought down by the Great Depression. Its elegant Pullman
cars were sold in 1939 to the Rhaetian Railway, where they're active today in
special-train service.

We rolled past the wood and stucco depot at Les Avants, a charming
chalet-style village where Hemingway hung out. Soon we popped out of a
tunnel at Les Cases, and there was fresh snow on the mountains. For the
rest of the day the scenery featured white on its palette in addition to the soft
gray of mist and rock and the hard green of trees. Beyond Zweisimmen, the
standard-gauge BLS train followed a steeply pitched river valley to Spiez, on
the Thunnersee. Since this would be the only one of the day's six transfers that
required walking more than a few steps, I was glad the rain had let up.

At Spiez, the *Blumlisalp* paddled into view across a mirror-calm Lake
Thun that reflected a perfect vision of lake transportation in 1906, the year the
vessel was built. As traditional as the *Crystal Panoramic Express* was futuristic,
the *Blumlisalp* had returned to service in 1992 after more than two decades of
inactivity. Her restoration was impeccable, with carved wood and polished
brass looking like new. Luncheon was well under way in the elegant dining

On a snowy, gray September afternoon, Breinzer Rothorn Bahn No. 12,
a youngster built in 1992, chugs steadily to the summit.

saloon when I boarded, but I was content to peer through the windows in the
paddle boxes to see the splash of lake water; to watch as the engineer, after
receiving the captain's commands through a brass speaking tube, hauled on
the throttle to slow, then reverse, the frantically flailing pistons; and to bask
in the welcome warmth and rich smells of steam machinery.

The railway station and dock are adjacent at Interlaken West; after a train
ride of just minutes I was at Interlaken Ost (East) and the Brienzersee—the
other lake that the resort city of Interlaken connects, or is "inter." There I
could have boarded the meter-gauge Berner Oberland-Bahnen to begin a 21-
mile journey to Jungfraujoch, at 11,333 feet the highest station in Europe. Or
I could have chosen the Brünigbahn, Swiss Federal's only meter-gauge line,
for the scenic run to Luzern. Instead, I opted for another paddle steamer.
Unlike the *Blumlisalp*, the *Lötschberg*—a near sister though newer, built in
1914—hadn't been restored. No need, since she had been in continual seasonal service since her launching.

The journey up the lake to Brienz took just over an hour, and I spent most
of it on deck in spite of the cold, enjoying the surge of the stream engine
below and watching the captain navigate from the bridge wing. At my stop,
Brienz, I crossed the street to the depot of the cog-wheel, steam-powered
Brienz Rothorn Bahn and bought a ticket for the 5-mile ride to the top. Two
modern red coaches with broad windows and plastic seats stood poised to
depart, ready to be shoved up the mountain by a chunky, green-painted steam

On a sunny day in May, mountains are still snowcapped as one
of the BRB's elderly steamers pauses during its climb.

locomotive, built in 1992 and thus significantly newer even than the coaches.
The railway had opened a century earlier, in 1892, and in addition to a quartet
of new steam locomotives built in the 1990s, it still rosters an engine dating
back to the line's inception, plus a pair from the 1930s.

With a lurch we were on our way at a slow but steady pace that would get
us to the summit, 5,506 feet higher, in just under an hour. Although mist hung
on the mountains, the vistas were stunning as I looked down on the rooftops
of Brienz and the chalky blue glacial waters of the Brienzersee. Little No. 12
chugged softly but gamely as it climbed the mountain. After looking up all day
at peaks clad in fresh snow, now I was looking down at them. Cold air stung
my face as I peered out the window to study the route we had taken—fragile
dark loops scribed across a blanket that was breathtakingly white against an
angry gray sky.

At Rothorn Kulm, the summit, I disembarked at dusk and shuffled
through new ankle-deep snow. It was the end on the line and felt like the
end of the journey, but I had to drop back down the mountain to get to Ba-
sel, where I would spend the night. The downbound trip as night closed in
was largely forgettable except for one thing. Midway to Brienz, we paused
so a hunter could sling a deer he had shot into the vestibule of the coach. It
steamed there in the cold, its ebbing body heat still sufficient to fog the cold
air. Fierce, impassive, bundled against the December-like September, the
hunter seemed to have arrived from another era.

No. 1049 on the Zig Zag Railway works back to Clarence Station, crossing one of the lovely sandstone viaducts on the "Top Road" of the switchbacks. (ABOVE)

No. 123, a 4-6-0 built in 1897, show its antique lines on the Etmilyn Forest Tramway. (LEFT)

11

GAUGE CHAOS DOWN UNDER

N THE FOOTPLATE OF NO. 1049, AN EX–QUEENSLAND
Railway 4-6-4T, Garth Schwartz hosed off his fireman's scoop,
heated it in the firebox, then dropped in some butter, followed by four fat
sausages. Soon they were brown and sizzling and fragrant. Pleased with his
ingenious cab cookery, Garth invited me to lunch.

Perhaps ironic, maybe heartening, but certainly intriguing is the fact
that my first experience with the time-honored but deeply obsolete tradi-
tion of cooking in steam locomotive cabs should have come at the hands of a
whiskerless teenager, "down under" on the Zig Zag Railway, a preserved and
sometimes steam-powered 42-inch-gauge line in Australia.

When, in August 1996, I'd boarded red-jacketed No. 1049 for a footplate
ride, I was struck by the youthful appearance of the fireman, who was indeed,
I learned later, a high school student. But by the end of my ride—a spectacular one, down and back through a switchback and across three long, elegant
fitted-sandstone viaducts—I was deeply impressed by the way he handled the
scoop and performed his other duties, perfectly in sync with Jon Rickard, the
driver, who *did* have whiskers. At the end of the late-morning round-trip, back
at Clarence Station, where we'd begun, I'd seen that Garth had one more trick
up his sleeve with the scoop—turning it into a griddle.

The Zig Zag Railway, a restoration of a spectacular bit of line in the Blue Mountains west of Sydney, is connected by suburban rail service with that city, a scenic three-hour ride away. Located just east of Lithgow, the switchbacks that made the Zig Zag Railway a zigzag were a remarkable feat of engineering when constructed between 1866 and 1869. This was the original main line west from Sydney, replaced in 1910 by a far more direct, less problematic route with 10 tunnels.

That old line had came to life beginning in 1975, when volunteers rebuilt a mile of track on the "Middle Road" of the zigzag; in 1986–88 more trackage went down, on the "Top Road," to Clarence. Though the railroad was originally standard gauge, the restoration was 42-inch gauge, presumably because steam locomotives were available for purchase from Queensland Railway—and just maybe to take advantage of some of the construction economies traditionally offered by narrow-gauge railroads, though in fact the right-of-way was already in place, tunnels and viaducts and all. When I rode, most weekday service used a QR motor-car set, but on weekends and school holidays steam ruled. The locomotive roster included a 4-8-0, a 2-8-2, a 4-6-2, and a trio of 4-6-4T's built in 1948–1952. These essentially bidirectional engines were ideal for the short hauls and quick turnarounds of Brisbane commuter service, their assignment on QR; that characteristic made them a perfect fit for their new role as well.

No. 1049 was one of the trio. In its cab, Rickard, a high school science teacher who has been involved with the Zig Zag Railway since its first year, hauled on the throttle as we set off from Clarence.

"It's always reassuring after I make the first application and know the brakes work," he said as we emerged from a long tunnel at Summit and nosed into the downgrade. "It's good to hear the air pump going. From here on it's all 1869 engineering," he added, "pick and shovel," as we approached the first of those lovely stone viaducts. Soon we reached "Top Points," the switch where the train reverses direction. We ran around it to remain on the downhill end. At "Bottom Points" we reversed direction again, this time to begin the climb back to Clarence. The "Bottom Road" of the original switchback alignment is the current main line from Sydney west; at a station at "Bottom Points," intercity local trains make request stops for those choosing to visit the Zig Zag Railway in the most appropriate way: by rail.

Garth had more work with the scoop on the upgrade haul, which in spite of his youth he managed with an easy assurance, still finding time to point out such sights as "Engineer's Lookout," a seat carved in the cliff from which John Whitton is said to have surveyed the work on his line. And then the fireman cooked sausages.

Somehow the "gauge-change operation" that the Zig Zag route had undergone seemed all too appropriate. Broad gauge, standard gauge, 42-inch gauge,

30-inch gauge: by all odds Australia must have the most gauge-confused railway history of any country in the world. What a mess! That being the case, the coast-to-coast railway odyssey Laurel and I made through Australia inevitably included some non-standard gauges—though many strides toward standardization had in fact been made over the quarter-century leading up to our travels, and especially in the years immediately before them.

Australia consists of six states plus the Northern Territory: Western Australia, South Australia, Victoria, New South Wales, Queensland, and Tasmania, an island off the south coast. These states, most settled as convict colonies, were fiercely independent, as they surely would prove in the matter of railway gauge. The Sydney Railway Company, building from that city, the capital of New South Wales, west to Parramentta, was planned by an Irish engineer, who brought a partiality to Irish Broad Gauge: 5 feet 3 inches. Surprisingly, Victoria and South Australia, also planning railways at the time, fell in line with NSW and ordered broad-gauge equipment.

But when the Irishman resigned in a salary dispute, he was replaced by an Englishman, who promptly abandoned broad gauge for standard, the norm in England; with equipment ordered, Victoria and South Australia pressed on with broad gauge, thus creating "break of gauge" problems that have been only partly eliminated. To further confuse matters, attracted by its construction economies, Queensland, Western Australia, and Tasmania chose 42-inch gauge, and South Australia built some, too. Meanwhile, Victoria built branch lines, "developmental railways," into the mountains in 2-foot 6-inch gauge.

Traveling east on the *Indian Pacific*—perhaps Australia's most famous train, linking the two oceans of its name—we understood both the problem and its partial solution as we glided by the station at Peterborough in South Australia, once an infamous triple "break-of-gauge" point, a dubious distinction shared with two other stations, Gladstone and Port Pirie. Standard, broad, and 42-inch gauge all had once converged there. By the time we passed, the multiple high-level concrete platforms were cracked and stained. The large waiting room, windows thick with grime and venetian blinds askew, was empty. A huge modern "signal box," or operating tower, was shuttered and dark. There was no one in sight. The *Indian Pacific* hardly slowed down.

By no means are all Australia's narrow-gauge lines excursion railroads, but a great many of the country's excursion railroads are narrow-gauge. The Etmilyn Forest Tramway, in Western Australia just south of Perth, the first steam preservation we encountered, was one that is. (In Australia, a "tramway" is an industrial railway.) While the Zig Zag's former QR No. 1049 was an example of late-era steam, built in 1951 and equipped with roller bearings, superheater, self-cleaning smokebox, and mechanical lubricators, EFT's 4-6-0 No. 123 was an iron horse of a different color. Literally, it was black, not red, and figuratively, it represented a far more primitive steam technology as a

A guard who works on the
Puffing Billy Railway
displays a token used to
control train movements,
in this case on the Belgrave
end of the line. (LEFT)

A train on the 2-foot 6-inch-
gauge Puffing Billy pops into
the afternoon sunlight at
Belgrave; levers controlling
switches and signals are at
 the right. (BELOW)

member of the Glasgow Locomotive Works class of 1897. About the only thing the locomotives shared was gauge, 42-inch, still common in Western Australia, on the state's Westrail system.

Based in the quaintly named town of Dwellingup, the tramway was part of the Hotham Valley Tourist Railway organization, which also ran mainline excursions (both steam and diesel) over Westrail lines. A decidedly modest operation, and the more charming for that, the tramway extended just 5 miles from the onetime lumbering town of Dwellingup into the forest. But with Clem Patchett's practiced hand on the throttle (he's a retired Westrail driver) and Bob Biggs handling the scoop, the century-old Ten-wheeler was all business as it worked back from Etmilyn, its exhaust sharp and steady, its banshee whistle shrill and urgent.

Up in the country's desolate "Red Centre," Alice Springs—an outpost that attained some notoriety from a Nevil Shute novel, *A Town Like Alice,* and the movie made from it—sees steam only occasionally, on the "Old Ghan." Train service to Alice Springs dates from 1929, when a 42-inch-gauge line from Port Augusta was completed. Prior to the railway's arrival, goods and travelers typically arrived in this outback city transported by camels imported for this purpose, driven by Afghan cameleers. In the early 1870s these camels ferried supplies for completion of the Overland Telegraph, linking Darwin on the northern coast with the rest of the country via Alice Springs. In the 1920s, camels were instrumental in the building of the Trans-Australian Railway (the *Indian Pacific's* route since the train's inauguration in 1970) and then the completion of the line to Alice Springs.

The Port Augusta–"Alice" passenger train quickly gained the informal moniker "The Ghan" after the cameleers. It also gained a reputation for tardiness and unreliability—well deserved, apparently, as the narrow-gauge tracks were prey to washouts from flash flooding, termite damage, and sun kinks. The journey, carded at a leisurely three days, often took much longer. Legend has it that the tardiest train arrived months after setting out.

In 1980, a standard-gauge line, running north from Tarcoola on a totally different route, was opened into Alice Springs, and the narrow gauge was abandoned, though 16 miles near Alice have been reopened by the Ghan Preservation Society for excursions. When we visited, this fragment of the original narrow-gauge Ghan route was operating with one of the distinctive NSU-class engines (built at Birmingham Carriage & Wagon Company but powered by Swiss-designed Sulzer engines) that served the line for many years. Stuart Station, located at MacDonnell siding, where cattle once were loaded, houses the "Old Ghan" headquarters and a modest museum. It was built in 1988 to the never-executed plans for an upgraded station at Alice Springs (originally called Stuart).

Puffing Billy, the granddaddy of Australian preserved railways, lies 26 miles east of Melbourne, at the end of the suburban Belgrave Line. Despite its whimsical name, the 2-foot 6-inch-gauge operation is highly professional, with 30 paid staff supplementing the 500 volunteers who make the operation work. In 1996, the traffic density varied from three to six trains daily, depending on the season and day of the week. All were steam-hauled, except on summer "total fire ban" days. Since multiple trains operate at once, the railroad uses a system of "tokens," which drivers carry, giving them permission to travel on a particular stretch of line.

One of four narrow-gauge "developmental railways," or branch lines, built by Victorian Railways around the turn of the last century, the line extended from Upper Ferntree Gully (about 3 miles south of Belgrave and the interchange with VR's broad gauge) to Gembrook, 18 miles. Traffic was lumber from Gembrook's mills, potatoes from local farms, shrubs from a nursery at Nobelius, and, right from the beginning, excursionists wanting to visit the lovely Dandenong Ranges. Closed in 1953 after a landslide, the line hosted excursions from Ferntree Gulley to Belgrave until that line broad-gauged in 1958. By this time the Puffing Billy Preservation Society had been formed, and in 1962 a different portion of the line had been opened for excursions. By 1975 operations had reached Lakeside, the terminus when we visited, 8 miles from Belgrave.

Primary motive power was five indigenous NA-class 2-6-2T's. Of the fleet of 17 used throughout Victorian Railways' 2-foot 6-inch system, the first two were built by Baldwin in 1898, while the balance were constructed on the same plans at VR's Newport Workshops in Melbourne between 1900 and 1915. Other locomotives on the roster included a Victorian Railways Garratt, then under restoration, and a Climax from the Forests Commission of Victoria. Together they made Puffing Billy a steam fan's paradise.

At Belgrave, we boarded the noon departure to Lakeside and return, which included a pair of handsome wooden cars (from the Mount Lyell Mining and Railway Company in Tasmania, so they required regauging for Puffing Billy service) with tables for meal service. Downbound, we were served a tasty and ample "hamper luncheon" along with pea soup, and on the return a Devonshire tea with scones, blackberry jam, and King Island cream. These comestibles vied for our attention with the lush scenery, rich in tree ferns, and the sights and sounds of No. 7A charging up Emerald Bank—all in all, a diet that was hard to beat.

On the *Queenslander* from Brisbane to Cairns, a run of 1,045 miles along Australia's east coast, the meals were even grander. This wonderful train, commodious and luxurious in spite of running on Queensland's 42-inch-gauge rails, was a weekly service, inaugurated in 1986. When we rode, the

Shortly after leaving the Belgrave station, an NA-class 2-6-2T
leads the noon Puffing Bill train toward Lakeside.

consist, which had been refurbished just four years earlier, included four
twinette sleepers with seven rooms each and two roomette sleepers with 12,
the *Daintree Lounge,* the *Coral Cay* restaurant, and the *Canecutters Bar,* plus
three "sitting cars"—chair cars or coaches, in Australian parlance—and a
lounge to serve them. The oldest cars dated from the early 1950s and the
newest from the mid-1980s.

   We boarded our sleeper, *Matthew Flinders* (named for a British sea captain
who was an early explorer of Australia), about half an hour before 11:30 AM
departure. From our handsomely appointed compartment—a fresh orchid
in a small vase was a keynote—we grabbed robes (embroidered with the
train's colorful logo) and headed for the generously proportioned shower
at the end of the corridor. By the time the *Queenslander* pulled out, we were
showered and felt reinvigorated from our moderately uncomfortable (though
in sleeping berths) overnight journey on the high-speed XTP from Sydney.
We headed for the *Daintree Lounge,* which took its color palate from the soft
blues and greens of the tropical rainforests of northern Queensland. The
Daintree featured a bar and scattering of plush easy chairs, plus an electric
piano. Playing and singing as the train pulled out was Nancy Grand, an American (given away immediately by her accent) who had been in Australia for
a dozen years. A talented vocalist, she was also the lounge's de facto hostess,
a role she relished.

A smartly uniformed attendant welcomes passengers aboard the *Queenslander.* (ABOVE)

The *Queenslander* restaurant car is ready for service. (LEFT)

By midafternoon we were passing sugarcane fields laced with 2-foot-gauge tracks plied by tiny cane cars.

"Queensland is the largest producer of sugar cane in the world," Grand reported between songs. As we progressed north, towns took on an increasingly tropical feel, with houses on stilts that let cooling breezes underneath and kept them safe from floods. Afternoon segued into evening, and Nancy Grand was back at her piano.

"If you haven't looked out the window lately," she said at cocktail hour, "there's a great show going on with the clouds and the setting sun." At dusk there was another show: the dramatic orange glow and leaping flames of a cane fire under a blue-gray sky. I thought *Götterdämmerung*, the Wagnerian twilight of the gods.

"Not very good for the air but beautiful to look at," Grand said of these fires, traditionally set to rid the fields of vermin, snakes, and poisonous insects before harvest. By then outlawed throughout most of Australia, they were virtually a thing of the past there. After the curtain came down on that spectacle, we moved to the dining car—a stylish room (rooms, really, since at one end of the *Canecutters Bar* was a restaurant annex) decorated in cool grays, blues, and greens. Luncheon out of Brisbane had been a scrumptious "buffet," with platters passed by the crew. First had come patés of fish, vegetables, and pork; then cold chicken, beef, ham, avocado, asparagus, and tomato; then meatballs, chicken satés, and quiche; then "mudcakes," fruit tarts, and coffee cream; then fruits and, finally, cheeses.

Dinner was even better. We chose a gruyere and artichoke strudel, then the cold "Whitsunday platter." Named for an island off the Queensland coast, this was a medley of giant prawns, smoked eel, oysters, salmon, and—best of all—Moreton Bay "bugs," a local crustacean akin to crayfish but, at least in that time and place, much, much better.

After a good night's sleep (though grudging; how could I miss those rail miles?) aboard *Matthew Flinders* between sheets carrying the train's logo, we ate and lazed the day away until our late afternoon arrival at Cairns. At Inghram we met the *Sunlander,* then a triweekly train on the Brisbane–Cairns route that was only slightly less grand than the *Queenslander.* Late sun made the final hour into Cairns exquisite. Behind lush green hills rose the distant western mountains, the Great Dividing Range, which is the spine of Australia. They loomed smoky gray, backlit by the setting sun.

The next day, a short ride to Kuranda rang down the curtain on a rail journey that had begun two weeks earlier—and it closed the circle, since the train I rode was at heart an excursion, like the Etmilyn Forest Tramway, which had begun our Australia railroading. The spectacular Cairns-Kuranda Railway, completed in 1891, crossed the cane fields of the Freshwater Valley, then wound its way upgrade into lush rainforests. Riding a wooden mainline

coach built in the 1930s for the Brisbane-Cairns *Sunshine Express,* I craned my neck out the open window and watched as we swung around tight Jungara Loop, then climbed toward the trip's scenic highlight, Stony Creek Falls, which we passed on a curved bridge over the gorge carved by the creek. Then expansive views opened up of the cane fields below, and the flood plain, and the Pacific Ocean.

Kuranda was lushly tropical. Waiting for the return train to Cairns, I sat in front of the 1915 station in the welcome shade of broad eaves, drinking a mango smoothie. Next to the station stood a trim signal box with manual-throw levers controlling all the small complex's switches and semaphores. The platforms were overflowing with assiduously tended gardens, including great splashes of poinsettia.

When I made my last entry—"21 miles from Cairns to Kuranda"—and snapped my notebook shut, I had traveled 5,827 mainline rail miles all told and checked out four narrow-gauge preserved railways. I had come a long way from the Indian Ocean—churned into whitecaps by the famous "Freemantle Doctor" prevailing winds—where we'd begun our rail odyssey.

At Kuranda, the train waits at the platform amid lush poinsettias for its return to Cairns. (FACING ABOVE)

Levers are manual-throw inside the signal box at Kuranda, the farthest extent of my Australian rail journey. (FACING BELOW)

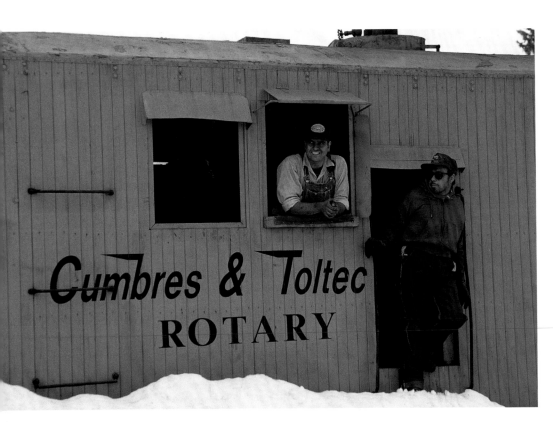

Beyond Coxo, the rotary snowplow and three Mikados work their way toward Windy Point. (ABOVE)

At Cumbres, Jack Campbell, in rotary OY's window, is relieved the toughest part of the plowing has been completed. (LEFT)

12

PLOWING INTO THE PAST

THE GREAT, GRAY, BOXY BEAST OF A ROTARY SNOWPLOW poked its fiercely bladed nose from the Chama, New Mexico, engine house of the Cumbres & Toltec Scenic Railroad. It stood silent and cold—but not for long.

It was about 1 PM on May 2, 1997, a sunny Friday still bitten with the cold of the departed winter. Boilermaker Donald Martinez scavenged wood scraps, rotted remnants of old beams and smaller stuff, and heaved them onto the fireman's deck of rotary OY, built by Alco's Cooke Works in 1923; from there, shopman Orlando Ulibarri tossed the wood through clamshell doors (wedged open with a lump of coal) and into the firebox. The boiler had been filled with cold water straight from the cistern, which came right from the Rio Chama. "Sometimes we get trout stuck in the hose," Martinez said with a chuckle. There was about an inch of water in the glass. "That'll swell to about three-quarters full when it heats up," according to Jack Campbell, the chief mechanical officer, who was responsible for the care and feeding of this rare specimen. Martinez shoveled coal on top of the wood in the firebox, then splashed in some diesel fuel. He and Ulibarri soaked wads of cotton waste in the fuel bucket, torched them with a lighter, and tossed them in after the wood and coal. "Wake up!" ordered Campbell. The firebox flamed to life.

Thus began the weekend of the rotary on the Cumbres & Toltec, a railroad that since 1971 has been hauling tourists over 64 miles of 3-foot-gauge rails that were once the Denver & Rio Grande's San Juan Extension, a line that originally ran from Alamosa to Durango, Colorado, zigzagging across the state line into New Mexico. (From Durango, branches reached Farmington, New Mexico, as well as Silverton.) In 1997, for the fifth time in that decade (and, as of this writing, the last time ever), the volume of snow over Cumbres Pass—the line's highest point and legendary battleground for men and machines versus snow, rich in stories of stalled trains and stranded crews—had led the railroad to fire up one of its ancient snowplows to clear the track for the start of excursion service on Memorial Day weekend.

This steaming of the rotary had many faces. It was a necessity, if C&TS was to begin hauling tourists on schedule. It was a railfan event, drawing devotees from as far away as Australia and England. It was a happening with a high profile for the local populace (and a considerable benefit for those in the hospitality business). It was a spectacle. And it was a huge expense for the railroad—about $30,000. To offset this, it had also become something of a fundraiser, as fans showed support by purchasing access to operating information and seats aboard an "escort train."

Above all, though, it was a remarkable survival of 1920s railroading, almost unalloyed. This was no sham, no show put on to entertain, like the pageants of Civil War reenactors. Here, the bullets were real. This was a gritty, problematic job that needed to be done and, it seemed at the time, could best be accomplished with a set of tools that happened to be more than 70 years old and pretty damn charismatic.

In the 1970s, C&TS, then under the management of Scenic Railways, Inc., its first operator, had on four occasions run a rotary plow just for fun. This was in the railroad's early years, not long after the states of Colorado and New Mexico had stepped in and acquired the line in the wake of its abandonment in 1969 by the Denver & Rio Grande Western. In all cases it was the OM, a plow slightly smaller, lighter, and less powerful than the OY; built in 1889 by Cooke Locomotive & Machine Works, this was the Rio Grande's first narrow-gauge rotary. Traditionally based at Chama for D&RG (and then the Denver & Rio Grande Western, after a 1921 reorganization), the OM initially remained there for C&TS, while the OY lived at the line's eastern terminus, Antonito, 29 miles from Alamosa.

Thus OM was handy (and OY totally inaccessible) when the railroad decided to go plowing in 1974—and again in 1975 and 1976, in all cases running no more than 9 miles east from Chama, well short of the rigors of Cumbres, which means "the summits" in Spanish and at 10,015 feet obviously is well named. Planning ahead for the fourth (and last, as things worked out) winter special in 1978, C&TS moved the OY to Antonito and made necessary repairs. This proved a lucky decision; in April, just a few months after the special, the OY was pressed into service to clear the entire line for movie work. This was the first time that Cumbres Pass had been plowed since 1962.

The OY was used again to open the line in 1983, a particularly late winter, but otherwise it lay dormant through the 1980s. Kyle Railways had taken over as operator from Scenic Railways in 1982; summer excursion business was growing to the point where locomotive and car maintenance filled all available off-season time, arguing against plowing snow for show. However, this growing business also led Kyle to expand its season in 1991; this earlier opening has meant more activity for the OY, which was steamed to open the line in 1991, 1993, 1994, 1995—and 1997, under the aegis of George Bartholomew, a new operator who had taken over from Kyle.

"Last year we didn't run it," Jack Campbell said. "The year before that we broke it." What broke in particular was the quarter shaft, which snapped in half, bending the main and eccentric rods and knocking out the front and back cylinder heads. "It all came apart in Los Pinos, up in the valley." Campbell and his crew had the OY rebuilt in time to open the line for the 1996 season, but it wasn't needed. In addition to the mechanical repairs, the rotary got new exterior sidewalls and a new coat of paint—gray, not the red it had previously worn. (Red had been the original color for the rotaries; along with other work equipment, they were painted gray in the 1940s. Both OM and OY finished their D&RGW careers in gray, but OY had been given a "heritage" red dress before making its first appearance for C&TS in 1978.) OM hasn't run since 1976.

"The OY is much the better of the two for cutting ice," Campbell explained. "It's superheated and has higher boiler pressure."

On the sunny Friday afternoon of the rotary steam-up, Chama was a wondrous place, a modest and traditional railroad town caught in a time warp. On an embankment, the main street stretched the length of the railroad yard. Facing it (and the tracks) were Fosters Hotel, dating from 1881, just after the railroad arrived in town, where the bar and restaurant have staunchly resisted gentrification. A block or so away was the Shamrock Hotel, built for Pat Kelly in 1939 to cater to business generated by the newly opened Gramps oil field nearby. Other buildings lining this quiet thoroughfare looked hardly newer.

The rambling board-and-batten depot, freshly painted in the Rio Grande's traditional yellow, stood across the yard throat from what's left of a brick roundhouse that was built in 1899, the same year as the station. Too short for "modern" power, modern meaning circa 1920s, its two stalls housed the diesel acquired by C&TS in the early 1970s from Hawaii's Oahu Railway and the tenderless 489, a Mikado then under repair. Tucked away behind it, the two-stall run-through shop built by C&TS in 1978 has itself acquired the patina of age.

I'd been to Chama before. The first time was in 1960, when Roger Cook and I visited briefly, following a double-headed freight from Durango. I was back in 1967, with Laurel, to witness steam over Cumbres Pass. This taste was so piquant that, in 1968, we staked out Colorado, desperately hoping for a second course, but it never came. Having filed in September 1967 with the Interstate Commerce Commission to abandon all its narrow-gauge operations, the Rio Grande ran as few freights as possible in 1968, citing mudslides and wash-ins that may or may not have occurred. I had been on hand in July 1971 to see the just-opened Cumbres & Toltec Scenic Railroad run a clean-up train, bringing freight cars to Chama that had been scattered on sidings along the line, and then in 1985 I rode a chartered caboose—0503, a wooden beauty built in 1880 that retained its workaday character—for a round-trip with family and friends from Antonito to Osier. Still I hadn't been able to lose the palpable ache of missed chances left by the summer of 1968. May 1997 finally eased that pain as best anything ever could.

By the time fire stirred in the belly of rotary OY in Chama, four locomotives were under steam, all husky outside-frame 2-8-2's, the ones that wrote the final pre-preservation chapter of narrow-gauge railroading in Colorado some three decades before. Nos. 484, 487, and 488 are K-36's, from among 10 built by Baldwin in 1925; No. 497, a K-37, is a slightly heavier Mike, one of the 10 rebuilt from standard-gauge Consolidations. Hostlers shuttled them here and there: ash pit, double-spouted water tank, sand house. Looming over the engine terminal was a massive wooden coaling tower, an icon of the narrow gauge, recently refurbished but not in service. Next to it was the sand house, where a wisp of smoke curling from the jack suggested activity within. Indeed, shovels rasped as workers tossed "green" sand into the drier. Fired up for the first time after winter repairs, No. 484 got checked out, running light for a few miles toward Cumbres.

As shadows lengthened, more and more fans gathered. Engines were sorted out and spotted for a night photo session. Then quiet replaced bustle. By the time the setting sun gilded the locomotive boilers for a final moment, the engine terminal was essentially deserted. In the Whistle Stop Cafe where windows looked out at the placid 2-8-2's, pony-tailed Alan Loomis served blackened trout to his customers. Two days later, on Sunday, he'd be brakeman aboard the escort train that would follow the plow east from Cumbres.

Before that, however, the rotary would have to get to the summit, a 13-mile run from Chama, much of it up backbreaking 4 percent grades. If the plow train made it that far on Saturday, the rotary and two locomotives would spend the night at Cumbres, with a single Mike returning to Chama to power the escort train the following day. "If I could tie up at 4 PM and get home in time for dinner, I'd be delighted," said Earl Knoob, majordomo of the rotary weekend. What volume of snow did he expect?

"When we get back in the trees at Coxo, it'll be 7 feet deep," he said. "The deepest drifts, probably about 10 feet, will be up on Windy Point." And what was the danger of rocks in the snow?

"Some."

Saturday morning, breathtakingly clear, was a three-ring circus under a canopy of coal smoke at the Chama engine terminal—four-ring, really, if you included the rotary along with the trio of K-36's (with the K-37 as protect power) that would propel it. In time the equipment was serviced and sorted out into the plow train that would head up the mountain: OY with auxiliary tender, Mikados 487, 488, and 484, water tank car, drop-bottom gondola with coal, an outfit car, and "caboose" No. 05635, a rebuilt stock car. (At its formation, C&TS had acquired just a single caboose from the Rio Grande, No. 0503, the car we'd chartered a dozen years before; at the time of the rotary operation it had just been repaired and was at Antonito.) No. 487, chosen as lead engine because it was equipped with a wedge plow, had Gerald Blea at the throttle and Jeremy Garcia as firemen. Aboard 488, the second engine, Jeff Stebbins (with whom I'd traveled in Ecuador) fired for Tom Atkinson, and aboard 484 Ulibarri fired for Carlos Llamas.

The OY, of course, was the key piece of equipment and one far more complex than its bland, boxy exterior, designed for protection against the snow, might suggest. Inside was a boiler much like a locomotive's, with a smokestack that reached to the roof and a steam dome. Reciprocating steam engines drove a pair of gears, linked to a third, connected to the longitudinal shaft that powered the rotary wheel. The wheel had two components: a cutting blade that sliced through the snow and a fan blade that flung it through a chute at the hood's top and well away from the tracks.

OY offered for its five-man crew a work environment that made a steam-locomotive cab seem the lap of luxury: Knoob was up front as pilot, calling the shots, along with Max Pacheco as flanger operator. Their space was largely bare of instrumentation: just a huge wheel to set the chute to throw snow right or left, a lever to drop the flanger down between the rails, a brake stand for emergency applications, and the all-important whistle cord. Marvin Casias, wheelman or rotary engineer, is stationed halfway back, on the right side, squeezed in between boiler and sidewall. The reverse lever, which controlled the direction of the wheel, poked up beside the boiler and the throttle sloped down from atop it. Looking along the boiler, Casias could see forward to the pilot's cab, where Knoob would be giving instructions by hand signal. The

Nearly to Cumbres Pass, the plow train climbs Windy Point.

wheelman had his own whistle cord; when he saw steam pressure dropping, he'd grab it and blow a single hoot, the signal to stop. Firemen Dale Aanes and Campbell (also the "mechanic on board") would work on the cramped deck in front of the tender, with few amenities other than fold-down seat, water glass, steam gauge, and injector.

Knoob had been with C&TS since 1981, when he went to work in the shop. He had served as fireman, brakeman, conductor, engineer, and train-master on his way to becoming superintendent of operations/safety and compliance officer. The rotary operation, with all its gritty excitement and stomach-churning uncertainty, was his baby.

"Better to have too much power than too little," he said, explaining the decision to use three engines plowing up to Cumbres. "If one engine loses its footing, the other two can pick up. With two engines you do it more with brute force; three just makes life a whole lot simpler. In any case, the trick is not to push too hard or else the blade loads up."

By midmorning, the entourage was ready to roll. Knoob's gloved hand grabbed the whistle cord in the rotary pilot's compartment, and two shrill blasts echoed off the facades of Chama's modest main street. Blea, Atkinson, and Llamas each responded in turn—a chorus in many voices, since each locomotive's whistle was as distinctive as a fingerprint. Then it was off along the Rio Chama, breezing through a stand of massive cottonwoods and then across open fields.

Before long the joyride was over, and the Mikes began lugging up the 4 percent grade. There was no joyride on paralleling Route 17 either, as the motorcade of fans, curious locals, and unlucky travelers who just happened to be heading east from Chama alternated between a crawl and a dead stop. The rotary train paused at Lobato so the three locomotives could split, each running separately across the trestle over Wolf Creek in deference to weight restrictions. Reassembled, the plow extra climbed and curved toward Cresco, where water was replenished.

Now all that was past was prologue, and OY and its three K-36 allies got down to business. Crowds waited at the road crossing at Coxo, where serious snow blanketed the landscape, making the exact location of the right-of-way difficult to guess. Announced by an advancing smudge of coal smoke, the OY inched around a tight curve, flinging a bridal veil of snow away from the tracks in an elegant arc. The Mikes slogged along at a measured pace; the rotary roared imperiously. As soon as the plow train cleared the road crossing, Knoob sounded a single shriek of the rotary's whistle to signal a lunch stop—a regrouping before the most strenuous work began.

Shortly after 1 PM the plowing recommenced, with the train moving across a meadow deep in snow that offered no clues on where it was hiding the railroad. Progress was slow with frequent pauses. For one thing, a main bearing on the rotary was overheating. During stops, the crew shoveled snow onto the cab deck; hatches were raised and the snow packed in to cool the bearing. Three hours after lunch, the assemblage had made it around a large horseshoe curve, about 2 miles in distance and a few hundred feet in elevation, and was tackling a big drift up on Windy Point, just a few hundred yards from the summit at Cumbres.

Observers looked up and watched the show from Coxo. As late sun washed the brown cliffs and cuts of Windy Point, the plow train hit the drift, backed up a few feet, then hit it again. Whistle signals came tumbling across the valley a split second after the puffs of steam that made them showed: one for stop, two for go ahead (or faster, when running), three for back up (or slower, when running). Occasionally the whistling was punctuated by reverberating blasts, as rocks on the track at Windy Point were blown to bits.

By this time Knoob had switched places with Casias and was wheelman.

"That drift was 10 feet deep," he'd recall the next day. "I had the throttle wide open and the reverse lever all the way forward. Each bite into the drift was just the length of the rotary hood, about 2 feet." It took 45 minutes to go 30 yards. Most communication was by whistle signal, but occasionally weighty news crackled over the radio.

"Four eighty eight to 487. Yeah, we're about out of water." Already running on empty, 484 had cut off so the crew could try—unsuccessfully, as it turned out—to get the pump working that would supply water from the tank car. Now 488 dropped off, leaving 487 to soldier on alone, plowing on to Cumbres and the succor of a water plug that stood shoulder deep in snow. Just as the sun was setting, the OY and 487 made it, throwing snow up on the hillside, away from the yellow clapboard section house. Nos. 488 and 484 limped in behind not many minutes later. Face dark with soot from his day's work with a scoop, Campbell stood in the gangway of the rotary, grinning broadly now that all the steam machinery under his command was safely at hand and watered.

As dusk faded to dark at Cumbres, the spectator crowds departed, leaving the Mikes to complete their day's work in solitude. Beyond the section house, high clouds in the western sky were tinged fiery orange, which deepened to rich mauve. No. 487 plowed out the passing siding east toward Tanglefoot Curve, then tackled the wye, working toward the remnant of snow shed that covered its far leg. Crews shoveled out switch points. Night fell, and 484 headed back to Chama to get ready to haul the next morning's escort train up the mountain. At Cumbres it was dark, still, and cold. It was May, but by morning puddles would be frozen over.

Chama was, by comparison, balmy when the escort train headed for Cumbres at 8:30 AM on Sunday under bright sun. "Today's format is free-form," Knoob had announced. "The only ground rule is that, wherever we are at 4:30 PM, we have to head for home." The objective was to reach and clear the new turning loop at Osier, about 28 miles from Chama and 15 from Cumbres.

No. 484 hammered its way up the 4 percent with five coaches and an open gondola in tow, carrying some 150 fans and locals who had paid $150 for the ride. Once the train climbed into snow, rail sounds were muffled. Passing through the deep drift at Windy Point, the coaches were up to their roofs in snow. When the train was stopped at Cumbres, a young boy reached out the coach window and made a snowball.

Out of Cumbres, Osier-bound, Knoob was at the throttle of the lead engine, while young Jeremy Garcia, a regular Antonito-based fireman during tourist season, wielded the scoop.

"It's much easier when you have gravity working with you," Garcia said with a grin, as the plow train headed downgrade across a broad snow meadow that revealed itself as Tanglefoot Curve. "They say a fireman earns his pay going uphill, an engineer downhill, making all the air sets," he added. "Per-

At Cumbres, plowing for the day completed, the last glow of
sunset silhouettes the section house and its order boards.

sonally, I'd much rather fire than run. I can't sit still." Belying his youthful
appearance are his six years with the railroad, more than half of them firing.
He started as night watchman in Antonito. Going to work for the Cumbres
& Toltec had just seemed natural for Garcia.

"As a kid I used to hang around the yard all the time. I knew Marvin, and
he would give me cab rides." Now Garcia was an accomplished fireman, one
who could readily explain the particular challenge of firing in plow-train service. "The harder locomotives work, the better they steam," he said. "Pushing
the rotary, you have to fire lightly."

"Once you get on the downhill," Knoob interjected from the right-hand
seatbox, "the rotary almost pulls itself through." Looking ahead from 487, the
crew could see the plow shimmy and buck as it churned around Tanglefoot.
"You can feel the vibration from the plow all the way back here."

The plow train had left Cumbres at about 11:30 AM, shadowed by the
escort train, which soon unloaded its passengers at the neck of Tanglefoot
for a photo runby. Going was slow, with frequent stops to get up steam on

Earl Knoob at the throttle of the lead engine of the
trio urging the rotary eastward from Cumbres.

the rotary. During one pause the fireman from 488—Dale Aanes, who had
worked the rotary the day before—walked forward on snow as high as the
locomotive running boards and stepped into 487's cab.

"Could I borrow a crescent wrench?" he asked Knoob, then went on to
discuss technique in firing the rotary. "My heel came 6 inches above the door,"
he said. "You know you have a good fire when you open the clamshell doors
and some coals fall out."

As the afternoon wore on, it became increasingly clear that the plow
would get nowhere near Osier, and passengers in the coaches grew drowsy.
Two days into the project, watching a rotary plow could be akin to watching
grass grow. After a final photo runby exquisitely lit by late afternoon sun, the
escort train turned tail just short of Los Pinos, backing the roughly 5 miles to
the wye at Cumbres and then heading back down the mountain to Chama.
The rotary plowed another mile or so, around the broad loop at Los Pinos,
before it too headed for home.

That evening, at the "Victory Dinner" at the Chama Community Center,
Knoob announced that—inasmuch as the day has been a moral victory only,
since plowing stopped well shy of Osier—coaches would be carried on the
plow train the next day, and all escort-train ticket holders would be welcome
to ride gratis as plowing was completed to Osier.

Later, the engine terminal was nearly deserted as a few hardy souls braved the chill to stroll among the hissing K-36's, watching the hostler ready them for another day's plowing. The coaling tower bulked against a night sky dotted with stars, and the darkness was alive with the traditional sights, smells, and sounds of steam railroading—almost exactly as it had been 30 years earlier, when common-carrier freight service was dying on the Rio Grande narrow gauge.

Guest Goose

Rarely has there been an icon as emblematic of a time, a place, and a railroad as the Rio Grande Southern's Galloping Goose. Conceived and built in the Depression's early years with the RGS in receivership and staring at a bleak future, these motor cars were home-made, half-baked, charismatic—and remarkably successful, breathing two additional decades of life into this frail and arrestingly scenic Colorado narrow gauge by providing mail, package express ("lcl," or "less than carload lots"), and passenger service at operating costs only a fraction of those for steam trains.

Built between 1931 and 1936 at the RGS shops at Ridgway under the direction of the ingenious Jack Odenbaugh, the railroad's chief mechanic there, the Geese, contrivances of which Rube Goldberg could be proud, numbered seven in all, although No. 1, which had an open, stave truck body, was scrapped after two years, apparently feeding parts to its successors. No. 2 was relatively small, and No. 6 was a "freight Goose" with flatbed body. The "standard" configuration—to the extent that anything about these cobbled-together, evolving critters could be called standard—belonged to Nos. 3, 4, 5, and 7, the articulated "big Geese." These had been built using Pierce Arrow limousine hoods, bodies, and (except for No. 7) motors, with large wood-framed, steel-sheathed "freight boxes" trailing behind to carry the mail and express

that were the Geese's real raison d'être. In 1946, Wayne bus bodies substituted for Nos. 3, 4, and 5's presumably deteriorating Pierce Arrow originals, and war-surplus GMC engines went under the hoods.

Through the 1930s and 1940s, Goose mileage typically outstripped steam-train mileage, and these silver-painted contraptions with the as-yet-informal moniker of "Galloping Goose" (for the cars' waddling gait on uncertain rails or the discordant, squawking honk of air horn) kept the RGS afloat long enough to haul uranium to the Manhattan Project—and to tote diminishing quantities of stock and ore through the 1940s. Over Lizard Head Pass they ran, both Geese and steam trains, across the Ophir trestles, up the branch to Telluride, through Trout Lake, Rico, and Dolores.

But the knockout blow for this railroad, marginal virtually from the time of its opening in 1891, came in 1949 when the U.S. Postal Service pulled the mail contract, leading to the suspension of scheduled Goose service. By this time, however, tourists had begun to discover the grandeur of the San Juan Mountains through which the RGS's 162.6 miles of slim gauge snaked and climbed. To cater to this demand, Rio Grande Southern cut window slots in the sides of the four big Geese's freight boxes, built in a concession counter to sell box lunches, and ran scheduled excursions in the summers of

Visiting the Cumbres & Toltec, Galloping Goose No. 5 is westbound between Osier and Los Pinos.

1950 and 1951. The Goose name, now institutionalized, was painted on the bus body sides, along with a nifty logo. But in spite of this brave, homespun initiative, the RGS embraced a fate half a century in the making and was shut down in 1952. With bodies and freight boxes stripped away, some of the Geese helped lift rail as the line was scrapped.

All six of the Geese extant in 1952 survived. No. 5 was given to the Dolores, Colorado, Rotary Club and put on display in front of the depot, where it sat for more than 40 years, deteriorating as inoperative vehicles exposed to the elements always will. No doubt few of the RGS aficionados who stopped by to see No. 5, or sister No. 4 stuffed and mounted at Telluride, ever thought either would run again. A few in the Dolores area figured that No. 5 might, however, and in 1987 they formed the Galloping Goose Historical Society. In February 1997, after a decade of dreaming and planning, restoration began. The society had decided that No. 5 would be returned to its circa 1951 appearance, which was scrupulously researched. For instance, a major dent in the lower bus body, souvenir of some stumble and clearly visible in period photographs, was consciously left unrepaired.

Its wooden frame hopelessly rotted, the freight box was rebuilt, reskinned, steam cleaned, and repainted. New rattan seats were fitted to the original frames. The all-steel structure was repaired or replaced to FRA standards. Wheel bearings were remachined, and all axles were turned. Engine and radiator were totally rebuilt. An army of volunteers contributed thousands of hours of skilled labor. The society's president, Wayne Brown, led the project to completion, which came in April 1998.

At the end of May, No. 5 was trucked to Chama for a week of excursions on the Cumbres & Toltec. The outings ranged the length of the railroad, a line richly evocative of the RGS in topography and engineering. The Goose ran well, although fuel-pump problems did crop up. Frequent gasping stops along the line forced Brown to prop open the winglike Pierce Arrow hood and minister to 42-year-old machinery, an appropriate reenactment of the adversity and ingenuity that typified the Rio Grande Southern.

On August 5, 1933, Goose No. 5 had flown for the first time. Construction costs totaled $2,599. Forty-five years later, on May 30, 1998, it had taken wing again. Restoration costs, strictly defined, totaled $78,200, although those close to the project feel the real costs were three times that number. In any event, few aboard or at trackside during the memorable week in June when the Goose was loose on the Cumbres & Toltec doubted that it was worth every penny.

El Tren de Sóller has arrived at the
elegant station at Palma. (ABOVE)

Passengers in the first-class compartment
await departure from Palma. (BELOW)

13

THROUGH MALLORCA'S MOUNTAINS

T HE RAILWAY CARRIAGE WAS AN HEIRLOOM, MORE THAN half a century old, pantograph-topped, with a wooden exterior. A pair of prominent, bug-eyed headlights looked as if they'd been borrowed from a racy automobile of the same period. Inside, our small first-class section was comfortable as an old shoe, although the seats—12 in all—were leatherette rather than leather, compromising the simile. The windows were open, and warm Mediterranean air wafted in. The wood worked and creaked as this motor car led its consist—*El Tren de Sóller*—back and forth through a slalom course of curves.

Many years before I made this ride, in 1978, I'd discovered a priceless narrow-gauge railroad—Alaska's White Pass & Yukon (see chapter 2)—more or less serendipitously while voyaging on a classic ship, Canadian Pacific's *Princess Patricia,* the main focus of that journey. The same good luck had occurred again, 20 years later, as Laurel and I sailed around the Mediterranean on another favorite ship of ours. Then called the SS *Rembrandt* and operating under the Premier Cruises house flag, it had entered service in 1959 as Holland America Line's SS *Rotterdam,* one of the last true ocean liners.

That summer 1998 cruise brought us to Palma, the port and major city on the island of Mallorca, or Majorca, off the coast of Spain, just across the

Balearic Sea from Barcelona. There I discovered *El Tren de Sóller,* the train from Palma to Sóller, the island's main tourist draw. It turned out to be an enchantingly traditional electric-powered railway, an ideal match for the equally traditional *Rembrandt.* A one-way ride on this train, which had become popular with tourists for its scenic route and the antiquity of its cars (and thus had thrived in spite of the highway tunnel that had been bored through the mountains over which the railway climbed), was included as part of a bus tour offered as a shore excursion to the ship's passengers. However, we chose to take the regular service train on our own, round-trip.

The Ferrocarril de Sóller, as the railroad is formally known, is a 3-foot-gauge, 17-mile line that runs from Palma de Mallorca across the island to the seaside resort town of Sóller. Originally powered by a trio of steam locomotives—named *Sóller, Palma,* and *Buñola* (this last an intermediate stop along the line)—the railroad was completed in 1912 with the primary objective of getting produce from the Sóller region to Palma and then electrified in 1929. The four handsome wooden-bodied motor cars still in use had been built that year in Zaragoza, along the river Ebro on the Spanish mainland, with Brill trucks and Siemens-Schuckert electrical equipment. The wooden trailers are of a similar vintage.

In Palma, we walked from the pier through the labyrinthine streets of the old city and across the Plaça Espanya to the railroad's ornate brick-and-concrete station, stately with its arched windows. Its manicured lawn, palm-shaded, was enclosed and gated with iron grillwork. The gate's tall entrance pillars, capped with round, frosted, illuminated globes, were bridged by an arched sign in Art Nouveau letters reading "Ferrocarril de Sóller." Vivid flowering vines provided a colorful backdrop to the station's single track. (Far less fetching was the adjacent station for the Serveis Ferroviaris de Mallorca, a workaday 18-mile meter-gauge line that operates modern cars to Inca, in the center of the island.)

We sat on a bench in the cool shade of wide eaves overhanging the Ferrocarril de Sóller platform as a crowd gathered to board our train. We had opted to travel first-class (only 545 pesos as opposed to 380 for second-class) so, as departure neared, we settled into the forward compartment of the motor car, the only first-class accomodation. To the rear of the car, beyond the toilet, was a second-class section fitted with slatted wooden seats, and trailers provided additional second-class space.

When the platform clock read exactly 10:40, the stationmaster rang his bell, the guard blew his cornucopia-shaped horn, and our train lurched into motion with the satisfying whine of traction motors and the squeal of peanut-vendor whistle. We slipped out of Palma with a modest bit of "street running" and then the traverse of the urban stew of light industry and trashed and abandoned stuff, from cars to sofas, before breaking into the rural plains lined with groves of orange and almond trees. When we passed a new station on Palma's outskirts, created for the convenience of bus tours, we were doubly glad we'd chosen to travel on our own. The downtown station was a far more appropriate departure point for this historic rail journey, and it would have been a shame to have missed it.

The little train rolled on to Buñola, a village largely unspoiled by tourism, where we met a Palma-bound train from Sóller. Then the rails climbed into the Sierra d'Alfábia, an impressive mountain range. This ascent took us across a five-arch viaduct and through 13 tunnels (one good reason for the electrification). Túnel Major, the longest at 9,120 feet and thus aptly named, we traversed in five minutes of dank, earthy darkness. Normal running time from Palma to Sóller was 55 minutes, but since the 10:40 departure was a *tren turístico,* our journey was carded for a little longer so we could stop at Mirador des Pujol de'n Banya to admire the view. From that lookout, it was barely possible to make out the station and church steeple in Sóller.

Then, as we began to descend, we clearly saw Sóller spread out across the valley below. Looping down, we could spot the tracks we'd shortly be rolling over and admire the neatly fitted drywall terracing on the mountainsides. We rolled through more groves of oranges, lemons, and limes. Descent completed, the motor and its little train came to a stop at the substantial Sóller station, but our journey wasn't over yet. Still ahead was a 3-mile, 20-minute ride by tram (also 3-foot gauge, opened in 1913) down to Puerto de Sóller.

This tram extension itself, and the fact that both lines were built in 3-foot gauge rather than the meter-gauge so much more common throughout the Continent and, in fact, the gauge of Mallorca's other railway lines, have intriguing (if possibly spurious) explanations. The story goes that, during the time of the Ferrocarril de Sóller's construction, government grant rules changed, making financial assistance available only to rail lines 30 kilometers long or more. As planned, the FS was only 27 kilometers, so the extension to the port of 4.8 kilometers was added, bringing the total to the required number. And the 3-foot gauge? Supposedly surplus locomotives from England built in that gauge were available on the cheap.

Trams ran every 30 minutes, so it wasn't long before one arrived—a pantograph car, one of three that date from the line's opening, and an open *jardinera* trailer that began life before the turn of the last century as a horse tram in Palma. We boarded, paid our modest fare, received from the guard a flimsy blue-green ticket marked "Sección Puerto–Ferrocarril de Sóller," and were soon on our way—snaking through downtown, traversing squares, and swinging by bustling cafés, then passing vineyards and yet more citrus groves. When we reached the arc of the harbor, beaches full of sunbathers were to

In the first-class compartment, the conductor
punches tickets, Sóller-bound. (ABOVE)

Headed for Sóller, the train swings out onto a five-arch
stone viaduct that is one of the line's highlights. (BELOW)

The tram from the port back to Sóller city center rolls along the harbor.
The power car was on hand for the line's opening in 1913.

our left and rows of shops, hotels, and restaurants to our right. We hopped off at a promising-looking restaurant with a good view of the harbor, had a fine lunch al fresco, watching small boats buzz about and the trams rattle by, then boarded a tram to catch the 2:10 PM train back to Palma.

As is so often the case, the return trip was a time for pondering and napping, the keen edge off the exploratory imperative of the outbound journey. Sun high, motion-generated breezes warmly caressing, we slouched in our padded seats, listening to the hum of traction motors and creak of aging woodwork. Before we knew it we were in Palma, with plenty of time to spare to be safely aboard the *Rembrandt* when she loosed her lines and steamed off toward Barcelona that evening.

When we strolled into the *Rembrandt*'s Odyssey Dining Room, itself something of a time warp, for dinner, I thought this: Isn't classic transportation wonderful?

14

A RAILWAY REBORN

A LONG THE BANKS OF THE BROAD, POWERFUL RIO MOTAGUA we stood and stared at the unwelcome boulders that had slumped over the narrow-gauge rails of Ferrovías Guatemala, blocking the path of our train. No. 205, a stalwart outside-frame Mikado built in 1948 by Baldwin Locomotive Works (think Denver & Rio Grande Western's very similar narrow-gauge power), hissed and wheezed, its pilot just feet from the rocks, while the crew, along with many of the 49 passengers, surveyed the impasse.

In fact, it was no big deal for Guatemalan railroaders, who routinely improvised their way through washouts, derailments, and other untoward events (up to and including the complete years-long shutdown of their railway), generally armed with only hand tools and their wits. Within minutes, crew members with crowbars pried boulders loose and wrestled them clear of the tracks. That done, engineer Jorge Diaz—76 years old, frail but indefatigable, and deeply proud of his locomotive and his work—yanked twice on

Early morning in El Rancho as No. 205 is about to begin the second lap of its run to the coast. (FACING PAGE)

The crew clears a rockslide near El Rico.

the whistle cord, sending sweet, shrill notes echoing off the hillside, which in turn sent passengers scrambling to reboard the train.

That was my cue to clamber up to the top of the locomotive's tender, where I joined Bob McLaughlin, a model railroader from Massachusetts, on a wooden bench wired more or less firmly in place.

"What a view!" Bob said with a big grin, unlimbering his camcorder. From this open-air perch, we could look down into the locomotive cab and watch Jorge and his fireman as they went about their arcane rituals—the subtle and specialized manipulations of throttle, brake handle, water injector, blower valve, and much else required to get an aging steam locomotive over the road. Or we could see past the locomotive's boiler and smokestack to the track ahead—or, for that matter, anywhere in a 360-degree orbit at the passing scenery. The 205 was an oil-burner, so there was no hail of cinders to contend with, though low-hanging branches could administer a nasty slap in the face.

Just as we were ready to roll, Barbara Coates, another passenger, hesitantly climbed up to make a third on the bench. "My husband will never believe I'm doing this," she said demurely, as we chuffed into motion, left the rockslide behind, and rambled along the Motagua at a stately 15 miles an hour. Speed, I found, is more relative than absolute. Fifteen miles per hour on a steam locomotive tender over marginal 3-foot-gauge track, rocking and rolling through the jungle, felt plenty fast.

We were on the second day of the weeklong "Great Guatemalan Rail Adventure," the February 2000 edition of a tour that Chris Skow's Trains Unlimited, Tours had been offering since 1988, in every year but 1999. Our journey would take us 197.4 rugged rail miles from Guatemala City, the capital, to the Caribbean Coast at Puerto Barrios, then back again, with some time out for sightseeing. One hundred and ninety-seven miles doesn't really tell the story, however; far more pertinent is the elevation differential: from 4,910 feet at Guatemala City to essentially sea level at the port. The western, mountainous section of this route is very much an up-and-down railroad, scattered with spectacular trestles and featuring ruling grades of 3 percent or better in both directions.

In fact, our trip was remarkable in many ways. Ferrovías Guatemala was an operation only about two months old, run by a United States–based concessionaire that had taken over a nationalized railway shut down for many years—since 1996. It's a story with many interweaving threads: Henry Posner's Railroad Development Corporation (RDC), the concessionaire, headquartered in Pittsburgh; Trains Unlimited, which for a few years operated the only trains on the line; the International Railways of Central America and Fegua, its nationalized successor; and the United Fruit Company, the giant corporation lurking behind IRCA.

The country's first railroad was the Guatemala Central, completed in 1884 from Puerto San Jose on the Pacific 75.5 miles to Guatemala City; it was chartered in California and built under the oversight of C. P. Huntington, its president, famous for his role in the Central Pacific. The line I rode, to the Caribbean, wasn't finished until 1908 as the Ferrocarril del Norte de Guatemala, the Guatemala Northern. By then Minor C. Keith, founder, in 1899, of the United Fruit Company, had begun acquiring railroads in Guatemala and El Salvador with the dream of a Central American railroad linking North and South America. In 1912, these lines, including the Guatemala Central and Guatemalan Northern, were incorporated in New Jersey, with Keith as president, as the International Railways of Central America, handmaiden of United Fruit (though bananas typically represented less than 10 percent of common carrier IRCA's revenues).

Although 3-foot-gauge, this was a big-time railroad, the most far-flung in Central America, totaling more than 500 miles and linking Mexico, El Salvador, and two oceans with Guatemala City. The shops there were extensive and impressive, though they were an eerie ghost town by the time we visited,

No. 205 struts its stuff running upgrade toward Agua Caliente.

seeming as if a huge workforce had just suddenly vanished (which I suppose wasn't far from the truth).

In 1950, four 1,000-horsepower diesel locomotives had been delivered by General Electric to modernize operations, but they sat idle until 1954 because, fearing job loss, the unions refused to operate them. The opening of the Atlantic Highway from Guatemala City to Puerto Barrios in 1959 was the final devastating blow to the railway, already tottering. Now trucks and buses expeditiously could haul the railroad's cargo and passengers. The year before, as the result of a 1954 antitrust suit, United Fruit had agreed to divest itself of its substantial ownership interest in IRCA. The railroad's last profitable year had been 1957.

For another decade the Guatemalan government propped up the line with loans; in 1968, with the railroad in default, the government foreclosed and began running the Guatemalan segment of IRCA as Ferrocarriles de Guatemala, or "Fegua." By then it was literally and figuratively falling apart. This decay continued until 1996, when Fegua threw in the towel and shut down all operations. By then, the line had deteriorated to impassability.

Trains Unlimited actually funded band-aid track work to enable its annual specials to operate over part of the line in 1997 and 1998. By February 1999, thanks to the ravages of Hurricane Mitch, it was beyond piecemeal help, and there was no trip.

Meanwhile, rebirth was at hand, and the moribund railway was privatized, to be operated as Ferrovías Guatemala by RDC. On April 15, 1999, the railroad limped back to life when a trainload of cement moved the 37 miles from El Chile to Guatemala City. In December the entire Guatemala City–Puerto Barrios line was reopened for freight service, and there were plans to rehabilitate other routes in phases: all the way to the Pacific at Puerto San Jose and Puerto Quetzal, the Mexican border at Tecún Umán, and the El Salvadorian border at Anguiatú. On February 19, 2000, a Trains Unlimited special once again stood at the Guatemala City station (or what was left of it, since a suspicious fire had burned out the head house in 1996), waiting to depart for El Rancho and Puerto Barrios—and I was aboard.

A nifty little train it certainly was. Behind Mikado No. 205 was coupled an auxiliary water car; a boxcar; a mail-baggage (*cerreo/equipaje*) in which a rudimentary kitchen had been fitted; a Spartan restaurant car (converted from a coach for charter service), where we would be served lunch daily and on one occasion breakfast; a coach with upholstered seats; and business car No. 1, *Michatoya* (named after a river flowing from Lago de Amatitlan, just south of Guatemala City), generally called the "presidential car." Even if highfalutin, this was accurate, since it had been used by two Guatemalan presidents—including the then-current one, Alvino Arizu, on the occasion of the railroad's 1999 reopening. Riding six-wheel trucks, this well-worn car had a writing desk with hooded lamp; above it hung a stained map of "Lineas de los Ferrocarriles Internationales de Centro America," a thermometer, and a barometer. There was a wrought-iron ceiling fan, a clerestory of green glass, a bunch of club chairs, two berths in the center, a galley, and—most important—an open, brass-railed observation platform.

In charge of the operation was Fernando Pombal, then director of Latin American tours for Trains Unlimited. There was no mistaking that our trip was an event, since Fernando was besieged at Guatemala City by radio and print media until engineer Jorge scattered the crowd with four warning blasts of 205's whistle. Then our train backed out, past the extensive shop complex. Poking their noses from the roundhouse were yellow-striped blue diesels that carried a stylized Zephyr-like Fegua logo, oddly sleek for this railroad, now ragtag but one that in its heyday had been a substantial and impressive operation. We turned on a wye track, then headed out of town. We rambled through the back streets of Guatemala City to a constant concert of American-style whistling from an American-style locomotive. Our route was packed with people watching and waving. As we rolled down one street, whores darted out of their cribs to see what all the syncopated commotion was about.

Beyond the city, trackside scenes spun by. A dozen women clustered around a spring doing wash. Schoolchildren swarming to wave at the train. Guards with guns. (Sometimes it was clear what they were guarding, sometimes not.) Endless warrens of cinderblock and corrugated shacks and later even bleaker ones made of sticks and black plastic. The poverty was palpable. Chickens, turkeys, and dogs were everywhere. Derelict shells of stations, concrete or wood, evoked a busier time, now well in the past.

After lunch in the diner—creamy cucumber salad, smoked ribs, beans and rice, washed down with beer ("Gallo Cerveza—*Famosa desde* 1896")—I took a seat on the tender to better enjoy the passing view. Before long I spotted a man with a rifle walking the tracks with his two small boys. He flagged us down with his red hat, to warn us of a train ahead, as best I could tell. Less than a mile further on, at El Carrizo, we came careening around the corner to find diesel No. 916 (Babcock & Wilcox, General Electrica Espanola, Licencia General Electric Company USA, 1971, from among an order of 18) on a trestle dead ahead. The 916 apparently was potential help for the 205 if needed. We stopped in plenty of time (no great trick at 15 to 20 mph) as the diesel scooted off the trestle.

From my perch I watched the men at work in the cab. Diaz had come out of retirement annually to run the Trains Unlimited special. Edgar Marroquin, the fireman, a full-time Ferrovías employee, was nicknamed "Chucho"—which sounds like choo-choo, though a chucho is a kind of dog, which was the derivation of the name. His father, who had also worked for the railroad, had the same nickname. Occasionally Chucho would cross the cab and grab the whistle cord; his touch was particularly attenuated and mournful. At times he would help Jorge horse the Johnson bar into the extreme reverse or forward quadrant.

"Jorge's stubborn," Fernando told me. "On the last Trains Unlimited trip, in 1998, we had gotten almost all the way back to Guatemala City without a derailment—another year we'd had 18 derailments, the grand tour of derailments, I called it—when we had a bad one, putting the whole train on the ground. It took three days to rerail the train, and Jorge refused to go home. He refused to leave his engine. 'I brought her out of the station,' he said, 'and I'm going to bring her back in.'"

We were greeted with universal interest along the way, either as royalty or as visitors from another planet, I was never sure which. Our passage apparently preempted whatever else might have been going on. Over much of the line, we were the first passenger train, and the first steam train, to pass in years, and hardly a single bystander ignored us. Workers in the fields stood as if at attention and watched. Small girls held tinier ones in their arms and stared. With our steam engine chugging along at little more than a walking pace, I easily made eye contact with individuals at trackside, which inevitably led to warm smiles and energetic waves.

"The way we're being welcomed is so touching," said Pamela Russell, a passenger who was taking her first train ride. "They seem so happy we're here."

Jorge made a good run, and we arrived at El Rancho, our destination that first day, well ahead of time. After an overnight at Hotel Longarone in nearby Rio Hondo, we were back at the wood-frame station at El Rancho the next morning. With early sun washing the scene, pigs moseyed across the tracks, and the crowd of curious bystanders grew. The Mikado took water, then showed off for passengers and locals alike in a photo runby. Because of our early departure from the hotel, breakfast was on the train: scrambled eggs, black bean puree, sausage, cheese, orange drink, Nescafe. All six waiters and cooks were friendly and efficient, but the dazzling smile of one, Gabriel, probably has persisted in the memory of many passengers.

"This was all washed out," Fernando said later, gesturing at a long fill at Rio Tambor, where the train had paused for photos. "Nothing was left but the bridge. Unfortunately, all the work here had to be done by hand." RDC had contracted with Pombal to rebuild substantial portions of the railroad. Working from October 1998 to July 1999, 150 to 200 laborers used the existing rail and replaced thousands of ties—five under every 33-foot length of rail (a new tie at every joint, plus three others). This, needless to say, was the bare minimum to make the track workable. To save money, sidings were left untouched.

"Repairs had to be done by train, since in many areas it was impossible to bring equipment in. To me it was a challenge," Fernando said. "Once we caught vandalism in progress. We could hear the hiss of cutting torches, as thieves sliced the rails so they could haul them off." Since one of the gang was an armed lookout, Fernando and his party quietly slipped away without challenging them.

"Most of the damage was done by Hurricane Mitch in October and November 1998," Fernando said. This was a serious curveball for RDC, which had been in the process of rehabilitating the line.

At Gualan, where we crossed the Motagua on a triple through truss bridge that had been corkscrewed by Mitch's floodwaters, we stopped to fill the locomotive's water tank. Here our coming was nothing short of a festival. Huge crowds had gathered on the station platform and lined the tracks. A truck-sized boom box blared Latin music. When we rolled out of town, whistle hollering and exhaust quickening, I waved grandly from *Michatoya*'s observation platform, feeling pretty important. And why not? I was standing where Guatemala's current and previous presidents had stood.

Waving to the crowd from *Michatoya*'s observation
platform as the train pulls out of Gualan.

Then, before long, we were stopped by that rock slide, which the section
speeder (or track car) acting as pilot had slipped obliviously by, not recogniz-
ing that it would impinge upon the Mike's greater girth. Fortunately, Jorge's
veteran eye spotted the problem in time, and the crew used crowbars and
brute force to clear the way.

Up on the tender leaving the rockslide, undeterred by occasional spatters
of rain, Bob and Barbara and I watched as No. 205 clanked through the little
town of El Rico. With Jorge leaning on the whistle cord, we swung around a
tight curve and again crossed the Rio Motagua on a long bridge paved with
rails that the railroad shared with the road. From the tender, the journey
was a scatter of chickens, a jog of pigs. Horses shied helplessly away from the
locomotive, straining against their tethers, fear in their eyes, and cattle were
attended by white tick-eating egrets in an exemplary symbiotic relationship.

Bananas obviously had played an important part in the history of the
once-proud, now-rickety railroad over which we were riding, since it had been

supported for many years by United Fruit Company, the archetypal corporate "ugly American." The line prospered as long as United Fruit prospered. Later history, however, is not pretty. Past Quirigua, we ran through banana plantations amid a high-arching spray of irrigators (since we were traveling in the dry season). Bunches of green bananas clung tight up under the spreading leaves. Here the United Fruit heritage was palpable. At Bananera, once United Fruit headquarters and the south end of that company's diverging line from Quirigua, we met a Guatemala City–bound freight: five flat cars of coiled steel (the railroad's primary commodity) and two cabooses, behind GE No. 902. We entered town by shoehorning through market stalls (roofed and sided in black plastic that could be folded back to clear the tracks), with produce and vendors literally but a foot or two away.

From there, only 12 passengers chose to complete the journey to Puerto Barrios by train, with the balance returning to Hotel Longarone by bus. Of that dozen, just roommate Rich Thom and I decided to remain overnight in Barrios and ride back to El Rancho the following day aboard the (supposedly) deadheading special while the rest of the group toured the Mayan ruins at Quirigua. We had envisioned ourselves having a leisurely morning saunter north, with the *Michatoya* all to ourselves, truly a private car, and watching the countryside roll by from the observation platform, listening to No. 205 chugging along.

As it turned out, opting to stay proved a decision of decidedly dubious merit. Fernando arranged a room for us at Hotel La Caribeña, where the engine crew was bunking. Their room and ours cost $21 total, which we were happy to pay. For $9 we had a very credible dinner of large prawns with garlic and rice. Our motel-style accommodation had no towels—but no mosquitoes either, happily, since we were in malaria country. Fernando said the crew, who had a six o'clock call, would pick us up and show us the way back to the yard.

Both our alarm and sirens seemingly right outside our doorway woke us at 5 A.M. I happened to spot Jorge and Chucho leaving, so we rushed out and trailed them through the drizzly, still-dark streets back to the engine terminal. There we climbed aboard *Michatoya,* where we found the train crew asleep in the berths at the forward end of the car, so we decided to go exploring. In the 10-stall roundhouse we found No. 204, sister Mikado to ours, a pair of pump handcars, and one of the railroad's newest and most powerful class of diesel: No. 1008, *San Marcos,* 2,000-horsepower, built in 1982 by Bombardier.

As the sky began to brighten from black to blue, we spotted a cut of corrugated banana cars, emblematic of the railroad's legacy; on the flanks of some, "banano" was still visible in faded paint. Nearby was yellow caboose G325, of which eventually we would see far too much. Yard switcher No. 700, a General Electric product from 1956, was fired up. It cleared its throat,

At Puerto Barrios, workers repair a brake hanger on the water car.

hiccupped, then began to purr. It was about then that our adventure seemed to be going awry.

No. 700 delivered our train to the turntable to be reversed, one car at a time. At about 10 A M another Bombardier unit—No. 1000, *Zacapa*—arrived from Guatemala City with one container, some 10 empty flats, and a caboose. A problem had cropped up the previous day, when a bolt on the brake hanger on one of our water car's trucks had sheared off. To fix it, workers jacked up the car, rolled the truck out from under it, removed the springs, replaced the bolt, then put it all back together again. By the time this was done, it was noon,

In a view from *Michatoya*, Bombardier No. 1008, *San Marcos*,
assembles the train at Puerto Barrios of which we'll be part.

and Rich and I were growing increasingly uneasy. Things weren't happening
the way we'd expected.

And then the reality became inescapably clear: the switcher was assem-
bling a freight train for No. 1008 to haul toward Guatemala City, and our
special, en masse, in tow, from Mikado through business car, was to be part
of it, along with six flat cars loaded with coiled steel. So much for listening to
the lovely, syncopated sounds of steam.

And what was that GE switcher doing with caboose G325? Pushing it
down the track toward us was what, until—with a jolt and clang of couplers,
and a stomach-sinking finality—it became for us a yellow wall, in our faces
as we sat glumly on *Michatoya*'s open platform. It, not *Michatoya*, would be
carrying the markers.

At 1:10 PM we finally left town. At Corozo we saw a string of banana cars,
most missing bits of corrugated siding, now no doubt serving as roofing for
nearby shacks. Overturned beside many dwellings were push cars with in-
geniously arranged flanged wheels. Clearly, since its closure, the locals had
begun to use the railroad for personal transport of goods.

Grinning little boys hitched rides. After dark these hitchhikers became more numerous and more unnerving—materializing out of the darkness, sometimes in groups, whistling and shouting back and forth, riding for long distances before agilely hopping off and disappearing into the night. By 11 PM we were trying to catch some sleep, but it had turned chilly, and the mattresses and bedding in the berths were damp with leaking rainwater.

Suddenly the train lurched to an abrupt and alarming stop. We stumbled out onto *Michatoya*'s platform to see the crew, whose annoyance registered with us even in Spanish, begin throwing tools off the caboose for others to retrieve. Rerailing tools. Rich and I were pretty sure we knew what the problem was, at least in general, but I walked forward to be sure. So I was not surprised to find that the last axle on the diesel and the first on the lead flat car had derailed. At 2 AM all wheels were back on the rails and we were under way again. At 3:45 we arrived at Zacapa, where a "taxi" had been ordered for us. It turned out to be a small, battered pickup truck, but we were grateful for it. At 4:30 AM we were back at the Hotel Longarone in warm, dry beds.

The next day, the first of two that it would take to wend our leisurely way back to Guatemala City, Henry Posner, RDC's chairman, rode along. Traveling with his daughter Ida, he was gracious in answering questions from passengers.

"This was considered to be an impossible suicide mission," he said. "As a project, it falls somewhere between a U.S. shortline and an Internet start-up."

If the eastern end of the rail route is characterized by lowland jungle, the western end—from Guatemala City to El Rancho, 65 miles—is a picturesque jumble of mountains, valleys, and rivers, which for the railroad means tight curves, stiff grades, and leggy trestles. Leaving El Rancho, the 205 tackled the railroad's steepest grade, 3.3 percent, and our progress slowed to a walk. We stopped, then started again. At first the reciprocating pull was painfully pronounced, but eventually Jorge had us rolling freely. (The problem, we later learned, was oil too cold after a recent refueling.) At Santa Rita, a dramatic locale with a long trestle and horseshoe curve, Posner and the rest of us unloaded for a photo runby.

"There's plenty of room for everyone. It's a big country," Posner said, then gracefully acceded when asked to move and join the photo line. The assembled photographers speculated about whether the wind might blow the smoke in our faces and spoil the view.

"We'll just have to wait and see," Posner said with a smile. "Sometimes you can't live a totally risk-free life." Time would eventually show the risks for his reborn railroad to be insurmountable. "It's more than a business," Posner would say as a valedictory to our group. "It's a cause."

But those developments were all in the future at Santa Rita when the Mikado backed up, then came charging forward under an impressive canopy of exhaust.

"Magic!" Pamela said. "And so full of anticipation, as you see the smoke around the bend—like a dragon coming. It takes me back to my Lionel trains."

In addition to first-timers like Pamela, our passenger list included some Trains Unlimited habitués. Dwight Long had 20 trips under his belt, and John Mueller 17—about 30 weeks all told. John had brought his daughter, Christine Milazzo, son-in-law, Joe, and grandsons John and Nick, five and three years old. All were having a ball.

On the last afternoon, rolling back to Guatemala City, Christine and young John were riding the locomotive tender when the train chugged through a tunnel.

"I gave up cigarettes six years ago," Christine said later. "But those few minutes made up for it." Not long afterward, the trip was over.

My favorite moments had come days earlier, however, on the last leg of the eastbound run to Puerto Barrios. Dusk had been closing in, which no doubt was why most passengers had opted to take the tour bus back to the hotel from Bananera rather than soldier on, in failing light, for the final 36 miles. The dozen of us who stuck it out were glad we did.

Most of us squeezed onto *Michatoya*'s open platform, sheltered by the overhanging roof from a light rain that had developed. The old car rocked and rolled like a ship at sea. Flirting with the Rio Motagua, now majestically wide, we traipsed through broad fields blanketed with fireflies. At every village, crowds had gathered, waving from cozy-seeming pools of light as the blue-gray world faded to black.

Eventually we sat in the pitch dark, drinking it all in: the fresh smell of wet jungle, the sounds of steam locomotive, the jostle of wheel on rail.

"The crew must think we're crazy," one of the passengers said. "Well, I guess we are." But none of us really believed it.

Brenda, a 19D named for one of Rohan Vos's daughters, shows off for passengers before departure from Capital Park. (ABOVE)

The interior of *Pride of Africa*'s "pillared" dining car *Shangani.* (BELOW)

15

WHERE NARROW GAUGE
IS STANDARD

WANDERING THROUGH ROVOS RAIL'S IMPECCABLY MANI-cured 25-acre Capital Park complex, just north of Pretoria, South Africa's capital, I thought of toy trains, but in one-to-one scale. Although full-sized, the trains there were in fact somewhat diminutive, riding rails just 42 inches apart, the norm throughout southern Africa if decidedly less than what the world calls "standard." Here was a trim, colonial-style station perfect in all details, seemingly newly minted but in fact created by thoroughly rebuilding a structure where apprentice engineers were once trained. Here were a dozen or so yard tracks, all neatly ballasted, hardly a rock out of place, which held shiny, spanking-clean cream-and-green coaching stock. Graphited smoke-boxes of highly polished 19D 4-8-2's poked from the far tracks of thoroughly refurbished run-through locomotive and car repair shops.

Capital Park really is one man's private layout. That rather extraordinary man is Rohan Vos (hence Rovos), who made his fortune in the auto parts business and is a lover of trains. As he wrote in a booklet published to celebrate the tenth anniversary of Rovos Rail on April 29, 1999, "At 40 I was well off. At 53, I'm broke. But boy, have I got a great train set." In the roughly dozen years that Rovos Rail had been running when Laurel and I visited in June 2000, its *Pride of Africa* had achieved a worldwide reputation for super-luxury service that retained at least a whiff of steam.

We were about to embark on its Pretoria–Victoria Falls itinerary, among the company's staples since it was introduced in 1994. After that, we'd go on to sample the *Blue Train* and (I by myself) the *Union Limited*. Ever since reading David Morgan's "Where the Trains Catch the Spray from the Falling Zambezi" in the May 1966 *Trains* magazine, I'd kept "Vic Falls" in the back of my mind as a must-do-someday rail destination. Thus I took notice when the *Pride of Africa* began making that journey. But, as it turned out, changes had come by the time we got there.

Fall flooding had caused major washouts in Zimbabwe, leading Rovos to replace the more or less straight-line Pretoria–Vic Falls journey with a wandering loop east to Kruger Park, then back west to Pietersburg—not actually all that far from Pretoria. From there, we'd be flown to Victoria Falls. Lost was a journey with a sense of destination. Gained was a more scenic route. And, further compensation, the flight would be on a DC-3 operated by South African Historic Flight, part of the Transnet Heritage Foundation.

There were reasons beyond the washouts that had led Rovos to the new Vic Falls arrangement. "Years of irritation with the railroads of Zimbabwe for delays and other problems," Vos told me. "Finally, I'd had it. Late arrivals wreck the theater, and that's what we are, theater." The last straw had been the derailment of 12 of the *Pride of Africa*'s 15 coaches being turned on the loop in Bulawayo. "Luckily, none fell over, and most of the passengers were off on tour," Vos said.

Arriving at the Capital Park station an hour before the *Pride of Africa*'s 10 AM departure, Laurel and I still felt a little let down not to be making the classic journey, but it would have been hard to stay disappointed. Passengers had begun to gather in the plush waiting room, full of overstuffed chairs and sofas. French doors opened onto a terrace, where, in a tiled mosaic, the Rovos Rail logo was at the center of a compass rose. Also in tile were signs with distances to endpoint cities of Rovos Rail's various routes: Cape Town, Dar es Salaam, Victoria Falls. A cellist and violinist played while train attendants passed champagne, orange juice, or mimosas.

Beyond a burbling fountain in the middle of the brick platform stood the graceful guest of honor: 19D 4-8-2 No. 2702, named *Brenda,* beautifully polished, with brass ornamentation gleaming. In its first years, the *Pride of Africa* was steam-worked for virtually the entire length of its trips, but that had changed as the infrastructure needed to support steam had been dismantled around the country. By 2000 steam had a largely ceremonial role, typically hauling trains only within a short radius of its Capital Park home base, for roughly the first (or last) hour. After that, electric or diesel traction ruled.

Still, *Brenda* made a lovely sight, steaming softly by the platform, on display for the admiring passengers until, as departure neared, she moved into the yards to pick up her train. Built in the late 1930s, *Brenda* carried a distinctive "Torpedo" tender, much like an American-style Vanderbilt tank. Riding on six-wheel Buckeye trucks (to distribute weight on branch-line tracks, for which 19D's were intended), these tenders, literally longer than the locomotives, gave the 19D a fine, rakish look.

Rovos had five operable steam engines, all beautifully restored. Three were 19D's, and one (the latest restoration, which included conversion from coal to oil firing) was a 25NC main-line 4-8-4. The gem of the fleet was a diminutive, ancient Class 6 4-6-0 built in 1893 by Dubs & Company and called *Tiffany* for Rohan and Anthea Vos's youngest daughter. (Her sisters, Brenda and Bianca, had 19D's as namesakes, as did her brother, Shaun. The 25NC was named for Marjorie, Rohan's mother. Such naming of locomotives is a time-honored practice in South Africa.)

Very much the hands-on owner, Vos was on deck to chat with passengers as they arrived, then formally welcome us as a group. (The morning before, when a train arrived from Cape Town, he had been there to help wrestle luggage. His office was on the second floor of the new station; from there he had a bird's-eye view of his train set.) We weren't that big a group to welcome: just 24, on a train with a capacity of 72. It was the last trip of the season, well into South Africa's winter, and political unrest in Zimbabwe had slowed tourism throughout southern Africa.

Departure from Capital Park was splendid. The morning had been foggy and retained a cool, damp softness, so the 19D was wreathed in white smoke as it curved out of the Rovos Rail compound. For a time the exhaust cadence was a slow, steady bark on an upgrade, but before long it became the satisfying roar of speed. The high-pitched whistle shrilled in its exhilaratingly foreign accent. I had the window down and, wearing the plastic goggles thoughtfully provided, enjoyed every moment of the brief steam experience.

Rovos Rail claimed to offer the most spacious rail-borne accommodations in the world, and who were we to argue? Our Royal Suite had a double bed permanently in place; a credenza with minibar and, below that, a tray with coffee and tea equipment; two easy chairs; ample closets and enough overhead storage for a pilgrimage; and a bathroom with not just a claw-footed bathtub but also a stall shower. This abundance of space was particularly impressive considering that trains in southern Africa run on 3-foot 6-inch-gauge track. Each sleeping car fit just two Royal Suites, so cars built to sleep 36 slept four. (Deluxe Suites, lacking only the bathtubs, came three to a car.)

In short, our room, in a car named *Limpopo* and paneled in dark wood, was equipped with every amenity imaginable. All beverages, hard or soft, were included in the fare, including those in the minibar. In addition to the

Royal Suite aboard the *Pride of Africa*.

Pride of Africa's observation car.

goggles, there were robes, a hair dryer, and a fully stocked toilet kit. Turn-down service by Lucy Brown, our hostess, included setting up the coffee for the morning, requiring of us just a flip of a switch. She picked up and returned laundry ("No charge," Vos had said in his briefing, "but please don't give us a week's worth of dirty clothes").

Rovos Rail had gotten its start when Vos bought a few cars to restore and use for vacation travel with his family. When he balked at the price the railway charged to haul the cars, officials suggested that he take paying guests. He decided to do just that and began accumulating locomotives and cars for refurbishing. First he rebuilt a set of wooden sleepers, later called the "Edwardian" rake and relegated to charter service. Some of these sleepers would be refurbished, he explained, showing us (on a pre-departure tour) one that was then in the shops. Next to it was a newer car, a second-class sleeper, typical of those steel-sided cars rebuilt for the "Classic 1" and "Classic 2" consists then running regularly. It was just a shell, with wooden floor removed and rusted metal cut away. It was hard to imagine its kinship with the smart green-and-cream sleepers that had been through the rebuilding process. *Limpopo*, for instance, though palatial when we occupied it, had been nothing special when built in 1977 by Union Carriage & Wagon.

"This is my last car to rebuild, my sixtieth," Vos said. "When we buy them, they're a mess. We get the floor done, then the electric and plumbing, and finally the paneling." It may have been Rohan's train set, but it was a big undertaking, with as many as 170 employees working out of Capital Park.

"The whole thing started with dining cars," Vos said, and they remained the pearls of the consist. The first, acquired in 1986, was *Shangani*, built in 1924, one of the wonderful "pillared" dining cars uniquely characteristic of South Africa's railways. Paired with a kitchen car (which includes staff quarters), *Shangani* took 18 months to refurbish. It was in our consist, and that first afternoon on the rails we headed there for a luncheon of duck and ostrich terrine, baked kingklip (a local fish) and banana with curry sauce, and chilled citrus mousse. Beautiful in dark wood, with ceiling-supporting pillars and arches, the car's paneling worked with a symphony of creaks as, behind a Spoornet (South Africa's nationalized rail system) electric locomotive, we headed east toward Nelspruit.

Our consist was Classic 1, without its usual midtrain lounge; this extra space would have been superfluous with so few of us aboard, and centering the sociability in the observation car was a wise idea. (Classic 2 would leave a few days later for Rovos Rail's annual 12-night trek from Cape Town to Dar es Salaam.) The observation car was a wooden, clerestory-roofed carriage cut away at the rear to provide an open platform backed by a wall of glass, allowing views from within the lounge section. In the course of the trip the car took on the thoroughly convivial atmosphere of a living room at a house party.

The scenery was good, with the drop from the highveld to the lowveld particularly dramatic. We were stopped at the picturesque Waterval-Boven station as the sun set; after four light locomotives rumbled through the yard, we eased into motion. There was just enough light to see the beautiful, toothy

The *Blue Train* exterior, seen here in 1977, looked much the same in 2000, though the interiors had been hugely upgraded.

escarpment we'd be descending in a series of tight loops: three dramatic whiplashes. An impressive waterfall shone silver against a blue cliff, then spilled through a series of pools. At full dark we reached the bottom.

The second day's scenery was even better as we approached Kruger National Park. We ran among koppies, pointed hills characteristic of the area; from the observation's open platform we spotted giraffe, hippos, impala, and monkeys. Meals in *Shangani,* drinks and talk in the obs car, and finally a wonderful flight by DC-3 over the remarkable Victoria Falls (much longer than Niagara and twice as high): not the trip we had originally bargained for, but first-rate nonetheless. And then on to the *Blue Train.*

"Good morning, ladies and gentlemen," murmured the speaker in our compartment. "The *Blue Train* is ready to depart. Will all guests not traveling with us please leave the train." Happily, that request did not apply to us, as we were settling in for the roughly 27-hour, 994-mile journey from Pretoria to Cape Town. Insulated from the far-less-stylish comings and goings of local trains in Pretoria's handsome station, built in 1912, we'd gathered in the dedicated *Blue Train* lounge, then been ushered to the train, where Fanie, the food and beverage manager, gave us a briefing.

"If you don't get, you didn't ask," he said. "Aboard the *Blue Train,* everything is free except French champagne and souvenirs in the gift shop."

With two bells announcing an on-time 8:50 AM departure, we slid away from the platform. We were barely moving when our "butler," a young woman

The Deluxe Suite on the *Blue Train,* with the
fresh fruit we found when we boarded.

named Hadi, dropped by to explain the intricacies of our room, and there
were some: a remote control that raised, lowered, and adjusted the angle of
the Venetian blinds (trapped between the inner and outer window glass)
and worked the TV, which on channel 1 showed an engineer's-eye view of
our journey; a cell phone to call her; and a temperature control with digital
readout. In addition to these high-tech features, the compartment—a Deluxe Suite, as opposed to a Luxury Suite, which would have included a CD
player and VCR, about the most superfluous gadgets on a train that I could
imagine—was just plain elegant, with finely crafted honey-colored wood
paneling of anigré veneer, framed by solid birch.

The bathroom, tricked out in Italian marble, had a shower (some had
tubs); souvenir robes and slippers were provided. By the window, on a table
that would fold out of the way at night, we had found a plate of sliced fresh
fruit when we boarded. Two built-in seats, piled with cushions, would make
down into twin lower berths at night, with a night table between. Alterna-
tively, some rooms had double beds. For daytime use, there was a third, mov-

able chair. Although the compartment lacked the showy abundance of space we'd had on Rovos, it was a perfectly conceived, thoroughly comfortable, fully convertible arrangement that worked well both day and night.

The *Blue Train,* operated by Spoornet, had its roots in the *Union Limited,* which had begun in 1923, running biweekly south from Pretoria via Johannesburg to Cape Town to connect with the Union Castle Line mail ships to and from England. Northbound, it was called the *Union Express.* These trains served the Table Bay Docks as well as downtown Cape Town and carried only first-class passengers and mail. In 1933 *Protea,* a luxurious new diner, was built for *Union Limited/Express* service and painted azure blue and cream with a silver roof, as was its attendant kitchen car. Initially the train's other cars were unpainted, with a varnished teak finish, but *Protea's* colors caught on, and by 1936 the *Union Limited* and *Union Express* had solid blue and cream consists. Before long, they acquired the nickname "Blue Train" and, in 1939, air-conditioned coaches in that color scheme.

Then, in 1942, these luxury trains were discontinued for the duration of World War II. When the service resumed in 1946, it had a new official name: the *Blue Train.* The next major milestone came in 1972, when it was completely reequipped with all new cars, two trains' worth rather than one, built in Nigel (near Johannesburg) by the Union Carriage and Wagon Company (Pty) Ltd. These were stunning consists, at once opulent and modern. I had ridden the *Blue Train* in 1977 and thought it the most elegant conveyance imaginable.

Much had changed in South African railroading over the two decades between that first visit and my return in 2000. Long-distance passenger rail services had been decimated until only a few trains remained, with most of these survivors drastically downgraded. Meanwhile, a new demand for up-market, super-luxury tour trains had surfaced worldwide. The *Blue Train* was reexamined in this light and the decision was made to rebuild the 1972 equipment, essentially creating a new train in an old shell. All compartments, now to be called "suites," would have private bathroom facilities, a relatively scarce amenity on the 1972 train as built. The first of the rebuilt consists had returned to service in 1997 and the second the following year. Work had been done at the Transwerk workshops.

So when we boarded the *Blue Train* in Pretoria, we found an astonishing opulence of décor—and we found butlers. Part and parcel of this elevation of service had been a shift in purpose from transportation to recreation, typical of luxury trains around the world. The *Blue Train* in 2000 offered a variety of itineraries: Cape Town–Port Elizabeth, Pretoria–Hoedspruit, Pretoria–Victoria Falls, and Pretoria–Cape Town, the original route. We had chosen this last one—for authenticity and for transportation, since we wanted to go to Cape Town. Also, the route was the southern anchor of John Cecil Rhodes's heroic "Cape to Cairo" railroad dream. The line to Vic Falls that we'd not been able to ride was another piece of that never-completed railroad.

The two *Blue Train* consists, each 18 cars long, were nearly identical, but only ours (trainset 2, with space for 76 passengers) carried an observation car, with an aft-looking full-width and full-height picture window, that could also serve as a conference facility. The view was good from there, but both the lounge car and the club car (smoking allowed) were more handsomely appointed. The club car contained a widescreen TV, allowing passengers at cocktails to see the track ahead.

At dinner, although the cappuccino of mushroom soup, boneless rack of lamb in pecan crust with BBQ sauce, and chocolate potjie with amarula cream (a South African liqueur) were all delicious, the service was scattered. When we returned to our room, on the other hand, we found that Hadi had been working efficiently. Beds were made down with puffy embroidered duvets featuring the train's sweeping *B* logo. Lights were dimmed and chocolates proffered.

At 7 AM, through the suite's broad window, the sky showed red-orange under a dome of ever-paler blue, ringed by black silhouettes of jagged hills. Now well off the arid, flat Karoo, we traversed a trio of tunnels (as seen on TV, by us in pajamas) amid a brushy mountain landscape that could easily have been the American West but was in fact the Hex River valley. We tried to call Hadi for coffee on the cell phone, but it was dead, so Laurel dressed and found her. Technology is wonderful only when it works.

After breakfast we headed for the observation car, where we watched the lush, mountain-backed vineyard and orchard country of the Western Cape roll by. Conversation was animated; a modish woman from Johannesburg who was Nelson Mandela's interior decorator held center stage—though, in fact, she was upstaged by the scenery spinning out beyond the wall of glass. Before we knew it, the morning had sped by, Table Mountain loomed to the left, and we were in Cape Town, right on time.

Though both were selling luxury, *Rovos Rail* and the *Blue Train* were quite different one from the other. The third of my trilogy of South African trains, the *Union Limited*, was more different still. It was comfortable rather than luxurious, thoroughly friendly, completely authentic, and gloriously steamy. From Cape Town, I rode (sans Laurel) the five-night "Golden Thread" excursion, swinging through the Cape's wine country, then taking the "Garden Route" to George. From there the train made round-trips to Oudtshoorn, over Montagu Pass, and then to Knysna on a famously scenic line that flirts with the Indian Ocean. Except when diesels took over for a brief, largely overnight stretch in each direction, steam was in charge.

A good deal of steam ran in regular service in South Africa into the 1980s. This had been the magnet for the two-week visit I made there in 1977, when

In June 1977, the *Drakensberg* steams out of Bloemfonatin on a chilly morning, bound for Cape Town. (ABOVE)

The *Drakensburg* diner set for dinner. (BELOW)

I scoured the country, mostly by automobile, with my camera, recording what I saw. Fortunately, many steam locomotives had been saved, about 75 of them in operable condition in 2000, in the collection of the Transnet Heritage Foundation, which owned and operated the *Union Limited,* as well as the *Outeniqua Choo-Tjoe* on the preserved line between George and Knysna, South African Historic Flight, and railway museums in George and Kimberley. (Transnet was South Africa's public transport company. Spoornet was its railway division and Portnet its maritime arm. The Heritage Foundation was yet another separate entity under that umbrella, as was South African Airways.)

At the Cape Town station, the *Union Limited*'s 11 blue-and-gray cars (including a refrigerated van for provisions on the rear and a "vapor" or heater car on the front) stood ready for an 11 AM departure. On the point was green-liveried No. 3407, a 25NC 4-8-4 built by North British in 1953 for service on the Karoo. It was originally one of the rare "condensing Northerns" that reclaimed water, acutely scarce on the Karoo, from used steam. That successful but high-maintenance concept fell out of favor in the 1970s, and the condensers were converted to conventional (non-condensing, or NC) locomotives. Thus No. 3407's tender (which had contained condensing equipment) was rebuilt at the Salt River works in 1978 into an ungainly "sausage dog" tank, so named because its low, long, rounded shape is reminiscent of a dachshund.

The coaches were as interesting as the locomotive, with the 1942 diner *Umtata* and its kitchen car (*Protea* also sees *Union Limited* service) and an air-conditioned lounge built in 1939 for the *Blue Train.* When the new *Blue Train* appeared in 1972, this 1939 consist had been decked out in a creamy pastel green and run as the *Drakensberg Express* on a zigzag cross-country route from Johannesburg to Durban to Bloemfontein to Cape Town—this last leg behind steam. I passed this up on my 1977 visit for logistical reasons, but I did ride Jo'burg–Durban–Bloemfontein.

I had found the *Drakensberg* (named after southern Africa's highest mountain range) a pure joy, perhaps even the highlight of my trip. At seven o'clock, Durban-bound from Jo'burg, I answered the call for dinner. As I pushed through the door of the dining saloon, I saw what seemed a stage set, an incarnation of my dream of dining in the great age of rail travel. Soft incandescent lighting glimmered off dark wood paneling. In the center, on a service buffet, stood an overflowing bouquet of fresh flowers. Tablecloths and napkins were of ecru damask; interwoven in threads of various subtle hues was the South African Railways coat of arms, with the Latin motto "Ex Unitate Vires." (This translates as "Strength from Unity"; although it undoubtedly stems from the amalgamation of the railroads after the formation of the Union of South Africa, it struck me as perhaps ironic in an apartheid

society.) Tables were filled to overflowing with a variety of flatware and hollowware: silver seemingly sufficient for two or three meals.

The profusion of silver had been to good purpose, for dinner did bear a resemblance to multiple meals. Service was table d'hôte, and the choices were limited or nonexistent within each particular course. The menu—or *spyskaart* in Dutch-based Afrikaans, bilingual South Africa's other language than English—stayed at the table, so, as I ordered one course at a time, I could project future capacity. A pawpaw cocktail had awaited me when I sat down; this I followed with mushroom soup, fried kingklip, a delicately prepared chicken, steamy sultana pudding, and a demitasse. With my table companion, a jovial, talkative Durban businessman, I shared a bottle of Nederburg Edelrood, a superb South African red wine.

After that sumptuous dinner, I returned to the lounge, where I'd had a pre-dinner scotch whiskey. It was this lounge, or its sister, that I'd encounter years later on the *Union Limited,* in the consist with a collection of sleepers, the oldest from 1936. Mine had been built in 1949 and contained five compartments, two coupés, and a shower. Since bookings were light (just 21 passengers), I'd been upgraded from a coupé (two beds, sold as a single in first class) to a compartment.

I had both compartment windows down as we accelerated out of Cape Town station under wire. The 25's are high-speed locomotives, and the roar from the stack and the urgent whistling got the trip off to a splendid start as 3407 hustled our train to Dal Josafat, a steam depot then owned by *Union Limited.* There we traded our 25NC for a pair of 19D's (one converted to burn oil) for an afternoon trip up the Porterville Branch through wine country.

"This is a journey of nostalgia for me," said Francois Ras. "I traveled on these coaches when I was young." Ras, who worked as public relations liaison manager for the city of Klerksdorp, also wrote for *SA Rail,* the Railway Society of Southern Africa's magazine. David McClure, owner of the private car *Indy* 400, was aboard and an enthusiast from Britain, but the rest were all just southern Africans out for a pleasant and affordable train ride. None were disappointed.

That evening the Porterville Winery hosted a traditional "braai," or barbecue, and wine tasting. Afterwards, back at the train, I was walking up to look at the simmering locomotives just as the crews arrived, chatting in Afrikaans. They torched some cotton waste on long handled scoops and thrust it into the fireboxes, then turned on the blowers and watched the sleeping 19D's come to life. Fireboxes became raging infernos. Generators began to whine and cab lights flickered and brightened, highlighting the brass of gauges and valves. We were ready to roll.

Back in my sleeper, I found that the "bedding attendant" had made up my berth. (On African trains, traditionally, bedding was rented separately

The *Union Limited* on the Porterville
Branch behind two 19D's. (ABOVE)

Tablemate Francois Ras is served aboard
Union Limited diner *Umtata*. (BELOW)

In early morning, the *Union Limited*, led by a 19D 4-8-2 and
GMAM Beyer-Garrat, storms upgrade out of Hartenbos.

from the room and bagged and removed each day.) From hostess to butler
to bedding attendant, I thought, the succession of my three train rides. This
terminology, like everything else on the *Union Limited,* was traditional. As
the two 19D's spoke in different whistle voices, I craned out the window to
see twin pillars of smoke glowing orange from the fireboxes and the coaches
stretched behind, their lights a string of pearls. I left my windows open for a
purposely fitful sleep and felt the cold night air flooding in.

At 6:45 the next morning I heard the rattle of spoons on cups in the corridor. "Coffee, sir?" asked Jeramiah, one of the waiters.

The days fell into a comfortable pattern: some off-the-train touring, at
least one photo runby (which even the non-buffs seemed to enjoy), and, when
under way, the constant background of stack music and whistling. Meals were
wonderful: unpretentious, freshly cooked, with the multiple courses expertly
dished out in the old-fashioned way, from platters carried through the car
by a succession of waiters. (Passengers felt so warmly toward the crew that,
spearheaded by a banker from Botswana, a scheme developed for us to serve
the crew dinner on the last night. Astonishingly, the dining car manager

Checking the fire aboard the Beyer-Garratt powering the *Union Limited*.

approved and we did it—a warmhearted and unintentional parody of their expertise, achieved with minimal loss of glassware.)

For most of the trip we were hauled by a 19D double-headed with one of Herbert William Garratt's eccentric machines: a class GMAM 4-8-2+2-8-4 Beyer-Garratt. Together the Garratt and the torpedo-tanked 4-8-2 strutted their stuff most dramatically one day at dawn, leaving Hartenbos and climbing the escarpment toward George, then later hoisting up the 2.8 percent grades through the folded mountains of Montagu Pass. There and on the line to Knysna, views were arresting.

It was fun just to be at George, where a completely authentic, fully functional steam-engine terminal was tucked within the wye formed by the George-Knysna Branch and the Garden Route main line. Engine house, sand house, and a "cocopan" coaling system (dump cars, loaded by hand) were still the normal order of the day on this preserved railroad, part of the Transnet Heritage Foundation. Switching and the line's limited freight service were largely by steam, though there was a Class 32 diesel (also part of the Heritage Collection) at work as well. The *Outeniqua Choo-Tjoe* hauled excursionists to Knysna.

The *Union Limited*'s cars did show some genteel shabbiness. They were preserved rather than restored. Being aboard I imagined to be much the experience of traveling South Africa's everyday long-distance trains in midcentury through the 1970s: steam on the point, good, hearty food graciously served, convivial fellow travelers, comfortable compartments with leatherette seats and windows that opened. I for one left the *Union Limited* with my hair full of cinders and a head full of good memories.

A Gauge Narrower Still

Most of southern Africa's railways were built in 42-inch gauge, which in fact became known as "Cape Gauge," after the Cape Province of South Africa. However, as I had discovered during my visit in 1977, the country also hosted a gauge considerably slimmer than its "standard" Cape Gauge: 2-foot.

Umzinto was headquarters for a dozen or so "toy" or "baby" Garratts that worked from there to Highflats and Donnybrook on one 2-foot-gauge line, and I had driven there from Durban to take a look. These diminutive locomotives were remarkable in a number of ways, beginning with their very smallness. So cramped were their tiny cabs that the driver's and fireman's seats swung out the cab doors, which allowed the crew to ride sort of sidesaddle, actually outside the locomotive cab. But perhaps the most remarkable thing of all about those little 2-6-2+2-6-2 Garratts was their youth; although the basic Garratt design dated from the 1920s, some of the NG-G16's I photographed were delivered by Beyer, Peacock & Company in 1967 and 1968, making them the newest South African Railways steam locomotives by more than a decade.

Hasty questions and half-understood answers at the Umzinto shed yielded this: A train from Donnybrook was due within the hour, and one bound the other way had left about an hour before. So I drove off to the northeast, increasingly edgy and lead-footed in the left-hand lane as I spotted neither train and the narrow, corkscrewing track, reminiscent of an amusement park railroad run wild, tantalized me with one perfect photo location after another. Finally I spotted Garratt NG131 with seven cars taking water at Dumisa. From there I followed this miniature assemblage on its winding, whistling course as it climbed the coastal range to the aptly named plateau town of Highflats, where it met a down train from Donnybrook and Ixopo. After both Garratts were serviced, they continued on their respective ways, but with crews swapped, so all could work their way back home. I watched NG86 drop down the mountain, then raced off myself, toward Durban, to reboard the *Drakensberg* for Bloemfontein.

Less than a week later I was back in 2-foot-gauge country, amid creatures almost as odd as the toy Garratts. From Assegaaibos west 70 miles to Avontour, trains were operated exclusively with 2-8-2 tender engines: NG15's, built by the

A "toy" Garratt climbs to Highflats.

Belgian firm Societé Anglo-Franco-Belge from the 1930s through the 1950s. A bizarre characteristic of these outside-frame 2-8-2's was their tenders, huge, boxy contrivances that hung low enough over the rails to obscure the trucks entirely—no doubt an expedient to lower the center of gravity and thus allow the tender capacity to be increased.

At Assegaaibos, the 2-8-2 on the morning train headed west with a commotion of rods, smoke, and sound all out of proportion to its size. Though small, this railroad was all business. About an hour on the way, the train crossed a carbon copy of itself, headed down from Avontour. Then a light locomotive, running with just a guard's van in tow, turned up, headed back from an early morning turn from Assegaaibos. At Twee Rivieres (Two Rivers) the 2-8-2 picked up a string of wagons and continued on downgrade. Though these little Mikes could easily be disparaged as dowdy, the valley they ran through was lushly scenic and featured some spectacular climbs. If anything, the photography was too easy, as if I were fishing for trout in a hatchery pool. By morning's end I had filled my creel with photos of these oddly attractive little fish and could happily go off angling for bigger quarry.

Behind a diminutive 2-8-2 with an out-sized tender, this 2-foot-gauge train from Assegaaibos is headed for Avontuur.

Double-headed Mal Tiempo 2-8-0's charge
through the cane fields. (ABOVE)

The shop force at the Mal Tiempo mill. (BELOW)

16

NEAR, YET SO DISTANT

SURROUNDED BY FIELDS OF SUGARCANE, UNDER A SUN-set sky streaked orange, the narrow-gauge rails stretched off into the distance. Along this track rattled a train of loaded sugarcane cars. At the head end, two ancient outside-frame Consolidations, built in Philadelphia by the Baldwin Locomotive Works in 1909 and 1920, struggled to keep the train moving. On the hind end, aboard primitive cabooses and flat cars with seats, 68 Americans held on tight as the cars banged through a switch leading to an *acopio,* or "reload," where cane was chopped and transferred from truck to train by a conveyor belt equipped with fans to blow off leaves and chaff. At the acopio, 11 miles from the mill, another locomotive panted softly, nudging cars into place to be filled with short lengths of cane.

In spite of the lack of amenities, these American passengers, I among them, were very, very happy, sitting on hard seats or standing, riding the 2-foot 6-inch-gauge rails belonging to Mal Tiempo, a sugar mill (or "central," as they're called) in Cuba's midsection. We weren't daunted by the fact that Mal Tiempo means "bad weather." We weren't troubled that, 15 minutes into our excursion, our train of reload-bound empty cane cars had broken in two; it was easily reassembled and we were on our way again. And no one was put

Mal Tiempo 2-8-0 smokes it up for an audience
equine and canine as well as human.

out that, on our return, with dusk closing in and the mill in sight, we were
delayed when one of the journal boxes on the sixth cane car in the consist
burst into flame, its oil-soaked waste ablaze.

So close, so inaccessible, so enigmatic, Cuba has intrigued a generation of
Americans forbidden to travel there. The island country's mystique has many
parts, and its attractions are manifold. Beaches and resorts. An accidental
museum of American automobiles from the 1940s and '50s—most still running very well, thank you. The earthy, infectious music brought to stateside
attention by the Buena Vista Social Club.

For those of us mesmerized by the rich olio of sights, sounds, and smells
that attend steam locomotives, however, they were an even more compel-
ling attraction. For us, Cuba had lurked for decades as a paradise just out of
reach. It was well known among the faithful that, each year in February, for
the annual *zafra,* or sugar harvest, a ragtag armada of locomotives steamed
to life to haul cane from field to mill—and, to a lesser extent, send the mill's
output on its way to customers, usually via interchange with the Cuban National Railways (the Ferrocarriles de Cuba, or FCC). A good guess was that,

in 2001, about 100 locomotives would be in steam for the harvest, although that number had been dropping annually, despite the resourcefulness of the machinists at the mills who kept these icons of another era alive. For many Americans, the much-remarked prevalence of ancient U.S.-built automobiles was emblematic of the Cuban make-do approach. For those of us in the know, the survival of the old locomotives was just as remarkable.

Canadian, British, and European steam enthusiasts had for years been beating a path to Cuba's metaphorical door, and by the turn of the new century more and more U.S. citizens—traveling illegally, through a third country such as Canada or Mexico but with increasing impunity—had swelled the tide. This illegality stemmed from an embargo enforced by the Treasury Department since 1962 under the Trading with the Enemy Act of 1917. It was not going to Cuba that was against the law; it was spending even a single dollar there. When Trains Unlimited, Tours—working under the umbrella of Global Exchange, a company that organized travel to difficult places—offered a trip in 2001, one that was totally on the up-and-up, licensed by the Treasury Department, many steam-starved Americans leaped at the chance to go. I signed right up.

Raw numbers were hardly the point, but they do provide context. Our group visited 13 mills, including one worked by ancient electric locomotives and one with diesels. We saw 27 locomotives in steam, all made in America, of two gauges—standard and 2-foot 6-inch. For economy, many of the lines into the cane fields had been built in narrow gauge, while tracks from the mills interchanging with FCC obviously had to be standard.

The oldest locomotive we saw in steam, at Mal Tiempo, dated from 1903 and the newest from 1925. Some looked as sharp as they must have the day they were delivered, painted and polished with loving pride by workers who saw them as emblematic of the owning mills. Others were bedraggled (if functional) hulks, covered with a leprosy of rust, with smokeboxes that rattled alarmingly as they chugged along. At one mill I watched a locomotive that I'd assumed to be on the scrap line as it was fired up in minutes to replace an ailing mate.

At two mills served by narrow-gauge networks into the cane fields we could actually climb aboard a train and ride: the Rafael Freyre and Mal Tiempo. In addition, we'd ride standard-gauge cane trains at two mills and spend a few days on the main lines of the Cuban National Railway (mainly in chartered American-built diesel railcars) and a highly memorable one on the classic interurban cars of the former Hershey Cuban Railway, now also part of the national system.

We participants in the "Cuban Rail Historian Tour" who arrived at Havana after a short charter flight from Miami were a diverse group. Most were serious railfans, though others just liked trains and were taking advantage of a rare opportunity to visit Cuba. Of the dozen women, many were spouses of those in category one. A notable exception was Mary Bill Bauer, a formidable woman inevitably festooned with cameras, extra lenses, and binoculars like so much outsized jewelry. She was an enthusiast through and through.

Getting right down to business, we visited two mills on our first afternoon in Cuba. At the second one, Gregorio Arlee Mañalich, which operated both narrow- and standard-gauge trackage, the neatly manicured property buzzed with activity. A standard-gauge locomotive (built by the Baldwin Locomotive Works in 1918) switched covered hopper cars—full of molasses, probably, since that's what most mills produced—to interchange with the FCC. As this trimly painted Mogul slipped its wheels, the fireman jumped down from the cab with a can of sand and trickled it on the rails for traction. The oil fire flashed in the firebox (all Cuban steam locomotives burned oil), throwing the engineer into hellish profile. The atmosphere hung deliciously heavy with the strong, sweet smell of molasses, an aroma I would come to associate with mills and steam locomotives.

Meanwhile, three fetching 2-foot 6-inch-gauge 2-8-0's (also Baldwin graduates of roughly the same era as their big brother) darted back and forth, shunting cars of cane, sometimes running over diamond crossings with the standard-gauge lines. From the balcony of the operations center where I stood and watched, it all reminded me of a wonderfully hyperactive model railroad. We hardly knew where to point our cameras.

This aura of model railroading was reinforced when one of the little locomotives chugged through an open switch and clobbered an empty cane car on the adjacent track, derailing it. Within minutes a front-end loader appeared and unceremoniously flipped the carbody off the tracks, then hauled the trucks into the clear with a chain. A foreman appeared with a tape measure to check the track gauge, and operations resumed as if nothing had happened. All this reminded me of nothing so much as the giant human hand that reaches down to lift an HO model off the track.

Cuba is a big island—more than 780 miles long—and our itinerary had us crisscrossing it on two-lane highways that were mixed-use arteries: buses, trucks (many with beds packed with standing travelers), autos of all vintages, bicycles, tractors (the omnipresent proletarian emblem), horsecars, oxcarts, cane wagons. Cuban transport, shaped by poverty and necessity, was nothing short of fascinating, whether railbound or roadbound.

Our frequent returns to Havana offered the best chances for tourism off the rails, and I was especially eager to walk in the footsteps of Hemingway. I visited a perfect little hole-in-the-wall bar and restaurant, La Bodeguita del Medio, where a trio played guitars and a clutch of young women danced sinuously in the "salsa" custom of the country. Posted on the wall was a Hemingway quote, "My mojito in la Bodeguita, my daiquiri in El Floridito," a

At Gregorio Arlee Mañalich, narrow-gauge 2-8-0
No. 1306 hauls cane cars. The tracks in the fore-
ground, worked by a 2-6-0, are standard gauge.

nearby watering hole. I visited both, drank both, then dropped in at Room 511 (now a museum) at the Ambos Mundos Hotel, where Hemingway lived and worked.

Best of all, a group of us hired a gypsy "taxi"—a Chevy from the 1940s—to visit the Museo Hemingway, his villa on the outskirts of town. This lovely, veranda-encircled building was virtually untouched from the day he left, with furniture and endless shelves of books all intact. Pilar, his famous sport-fishing boat, was on the grounds. The bad news: The museum was entirely uninterpreted (in any language) by signs or docents, and it could be viewed only through open windows.

From Havana we headed east to the coastal resort town of Guardalavaca. Three nights there allowed the less steam-obsessed to swim in the expansive pool or ocean and relax, while most of us trekked to the nearby Rafael Freyre mill for two days of charter trips over its extensive narrow-gauge railroad. For the first time since the nationalization of the mills after the revolution, the Freyre mill was shut because of poor harvest—a disappointment, though it

The Rafael Freyre is the most extensive and
scenic of Cuba's narrow-gauge cane lines.

did allow us to tour the mill building itself, off limits at any working facility.
These mills, steam-powered, were in the same time warp as the locomotives.
The machinery at Rafael Freyre dated from 1914 to 1919.

The mill's closure deprived us of quite a show: 30 trains daily at operational peaks over 50 miles of track, which would have kept seven little Baldwin 2-8-0's, built in Philadelphia from 1905 to 1919, plenty busy, along with
some Russian diesels. Happily, though, charters were operated just for us.
They were leisurely jogs that offered a welcome window on rural Cuba. With
the sweet notes of the steam whistle heralding our coming, punctuating the
limping cadence of the locomotive's exhaust, testimony that its valves were
out of true, we passed boys throwing a much-repaired baseball (I wished
I'd brought a new one along to toss to them as we rolled by), all manner of
animal-powered transport, and, at each modest settlement, clusters of townspeople waving. We saw a ballpark with goats grazing in the outfield.

At Potrerillo, the end of one branch line, I watched a haircut in progress
on a trackside porch. On the way back to the mill, we stopped at a small,
traditional tobacco farm with a thatched-roof drying shed. The host handed

out cigars. Speeds were not great. When a passenger dropped his camera case overboard, the engineer spotted it—then, without fuss, backed up to retrieve it. Wearing a black Nike T-shirt, youthful Miraluis Zaldivar—Cuba's only female locomotive engineer, qualified on steam as well as diesel—had fired on our morning excursion. Now back at Rafael Freyre, she was on the little porch of the crew room, boogying with a few coworkers to some boom box salsa. They responded with forbearance when I joined in.

Our last whiff of steam came on the standard-gauge rails of the Venezuela mill, where we highballed out into the cane fields aboard four bright-orange cabooses behind an immaculately maintained 2-8-0. Afterward, buses waited to whisk us back to our hotel, but a dozen of us opted for a slower return aboard the FCC charter train that had brought us: a string of Romanian boxcars converted to marginal coaches by the addition of windows and folding bus doors. A few bare bulbs dangling from the ceiling provided just enough light for me to find and pop a last, warm *cerveza*.

Exhilarating and clamorous, the ride back was, oddly enough, a highlight—cars slamming and banging, diesel horn wailing insistently. I sat on the steps with the doors pushed aside as the train surged through the fragrant darkness of cane fields, then slowed for towns, where the front room of each modest home glowed with the blue of black-and-white TV. The air was luxurious, the cool of evening just right after a hot day in the sun.

And this particular American was still very, very happy.

A saloon car and toast-rack trailer—seen here rolling through Fairy Cottage, Douglas-bound in 2003—are the most typical combination of cars on the Manx Electric Railway. (ABOVE)

At Laxey, the lower terminal for the Snaefell Mountain Railway, motormen converse in front of cars dating from 1895. (BELOW)

17

RAILWAY BRIGADOON

I'LL BET JEFF IS DRIVING," SAID THE ELDERLY, SNAGGLE-toothed woman who shared our snug six-seat compartment. Swaying energetically from side to side, the little wooden railway carriage in which we rode banged loudly over opposed rail joints, which sang "ka-*chunk*, ka-*chunk*" instead of the clickety-clack of staggered (American-style) joints. Up ahead a diminutive steam locomotive chugged gamely. "They call Jeff the 'mad driver,'" she added. Outside the window, held open by a well-worn leather strap, a green pastoral landscape scrolled by at a stately pace, with occasional glimpses of blue sea as punctuation. Warm afternoon air wafted in, carrying the smell of cows—and of coal smoke, rolling back from the locomotive.

We paused at Ballasalla, a modest station where a handful of women disembarked, burdened with shopping bags. "*Ballasalla* means 'small settlement,'" said our chatty compartment-mate, who was also on her way home from a shopping trip. Then came the sequential bangs as the guard secured the "slam-door" cars before signaling departure with his green flag. With a shrill squeal of its "peanut-vendor" whistle, our engine lurched into motion, shuffling away from Ballasalla with the chant of exhaust that always announces the passage of steam locomotives.

The year was not 1874, when the 3-foot-gauge line over which we traveled was completed. It was not 1905, when famed British builder Beyer, Peacock & Company delivered the locomotive up ahead—No. 10, the *G. H. Wood*, a 2-4-0T. It was not even 1923, when our little compartment coach with plush seats and brass hat racks was constructed. It was, in fact, 2003, and the place was the Isle of Man. A small (12 by 30 miles) island plunked in the middle of the Irish Sea, roughly equidistant from Scotland, England, and Northern Ireland, it's a sort of transportation Brigadoon, a place that seems to have just awakened, as if by magic, after a century's slumber.

Man is in many ways an eccentric isle. Manx cats are tailless. The Tynwald, the independent Manx legislature (though the island is essentially part of Great Britain), is the oldest continuously sitting governing body in the world. The Vikings established it in 979. Offshore money piles up on the island. Each June, during the long-established T.T. (Tourist Trophy) Races, motorcycles careen around the largely rural island's curvy, hilly roads. Years ago, when motorcycle racing was in its infancy, the Manx chose to waive speed limits, a concession the British were unwilling to make. This easy attitude, coupled with the island's mountainous terrain, established biking as an integral, if somewhat paradoxical, aspect of Manx life.

However, the insular eccentricity that most endears the Isle of Man to me is its rail transport, which comes in five flavors—all succulent, each distinctive, all ancient and undersized. There's the 15.5-mile steam-powered Isle of Man Railway, which we traveled with the friendly shopper. The only surviving remnant of a larger steam-railway system, it now connects the capital city of Douglas with Port Erin at the island's southwest corner.

There's the Manx Electric Railway, an interurban line that runs its scenic 17.5-mile course from Douglas to Ramsey on the northeast coast. Roughly halfway along, at Laxey, a mountain railway, also electrified, takes off to climb to the 2,034-foot summit of Snaefell Mountain. Along the Promenade in Douglas runs a horse-powered tramway. And if these are not enough small, elderly trains for you, try the even tinier, once-abandoned Groudle Glen Railway, built in 1896 to carry visitors to a now-long-defunct zoo; it was restored by enthusiasts and reopened beginning in 1986.

All this turned a rail buff like me into a kid in a candy shop.

Laurel, Rich Taylor, and I arrived at Douglas at nightfall in July 2003. We were aboard a vessel of the Isle of Man Steam Packet Company. Dating from 1830, this line retains its quintessentially evocative name and classic house flag, featuring the pinwheel-like, three-legged Manx herald. However, the vessel of our crossing—a two-hour, 30-minute trip from Liverpool—was the *Seacat Isle of Man,* an uninspiring catamaran. This mostly enclosed projectile unhappily combined a buslike sterility with advancing shoddiness. Still, Douglas Head and the Loch Promenade, twinkling with decorative lights and lined with an arc of ornate buildings, predominantly Victorian, looked fetching in the blue hour of dusk as we slid into the harbor. The town seemed the archetype of a working-class English seaside resort. That's how Laurel and I remembered it from our only previous visit, in 1970.

On that occasion, we'd arrived far more grandly, if more slowly, aboard the Steam Packet Company's *Manxman,* built in 1955. It was one of the eight twin-screw vessels, powered by steam turbines, that the line then operated to serve various ports on routes radiating from Douglas—to Ardrossan and to Belfast, as well as the Princess Landing Stage in Liverpool, our departure point. All the vessels looked like miniature Cunard liners, with fine, traditional profiles and nearly identical funnel markings—black-banded red. When questioned on the similarity, Packet Company officials merely pointed out that their claim to the colors was older. (Cunard Line dates from 1840.)

The matriarch of the Isle of Man fleet was the elegant *Lady of Mann,* known as the "Centenary Steamer" because she was launched in 1930, the company's hundredth anniversary. This vessel, the line's largest in both ton-

The lovely *Lady of Mann,* launched in 1930, was still steaming in 1970 for the Isle of Man Steam Packet Company.

The platform awnings are in place at the Douglas terminal of the Isle of Man Railway in 1970. Happily, No. 19, the *G. H. Wood,* was still there when we returned in 2003, although the awnings weren't. (ABOVE)

The grand brick head house of the Douglas terminal, seen here in 1970, has survived. (BELOW)

nage and passenger capacity, was particularly handsome, featuring a distinctive wooden bridge. The newest vessels were *Manx Maid* (1962) and *Ben-My-Chree* (1965), which looked like classic liners in spite of being car ferries. Other vessels included the *Tynewald, Mona's Isle, Snaefell,* and *King Orry*. We saw most of them during our stay on the island.

Much more had changed on the Isle of Man over the three decades between our visits than the style of the vessels that serve it. For one thing, the island had lost much of its luster as a seaside resort. But probably the thing that had changed the least was its transportation system. Not that it hadn't been in some peril. In the mid-1970s, for instance, the Manx Electric was especially shaky, and the north end of the line actually was shut down for one season. However, extensive centennial celebrations in 1993 shone a bright spotlight on the line in a helpful way.

True, a few things I looked for when we returned in 2003 were gone. An ornate canopy at the Derby Castle end of the horse tramway had been torn down in 1980. An evocative and quintessentially Victorian structure, the brick head house of the steam railway's Douglas terminus still stood proud; however, the platform awnings had been removed—along with the coach yard and engine shed and some of the station tracks—to make room for bus parking.

For the most part, though, the change that has come to the Isle of Man Railway Company largely predates 1970. Founded exactly a century before that year of our first visit, the railway once comprised lines from Douglas northwest to Peel (the first opened, in 1873), southwest to Port Erin (the second opened, in 1874, and only surviving), and north via the west coast (opened in 1879 as the Manx Northern Railway) to Ramsey, also the northern terminus of the Manx Electric Railway. Operating largely with original locomotives and rolling stock, the steam trains remained an essential element of transportation on the island well into the 1950s. By the 1960s, in common with branch lines throughout Britain, the railroad saw patronage dwindle. Beginning in 1960, winter closures began. In the fall of 1965, the entire system shut down for the winter, and Isle of Man Railway's permanent closure was soon announced.

By then, happily, the recently established Transport Commission recognized its tourism potential, and the line to Port Erin reopened in June 1967 for seasonal service, which we sampled in both 1970 and 2003. In both cases we rode behind No. 10, which was clad in green on the earlier occasion and brown on the latter, always shiny, with brass dome gleaming. On the second visit No. 15, *Caledonia*, the line's only 0-6-0T, was also in steam; this Dübs & Company tanker dates from 1885.

On the first morning of our 2003 visit, the three of us walked north along the Promenade to Derby Castle, the Douglas terminus of the deliciously an-

Car No. 2, an "unvestibuled saloon car" built
in 1893, pauses briefly at South Cape.

cient Manx Electric Railway. Of all the island's flanged-wheel glories, for me
the MER is the most glorious. The line, 3-foot-gauge like the steam railway,
runs along the east coast, flirting with the Irish Sea for much of the way, often from high cliffs. This topography translated to grades too steep for steam
locomotives, so the railway was built as an electric interurban.

An interurban—sort of a streetcar on steroids—runs between cities
rather than within them, of course, hence the name. Once common in the
United States, interurbans were rare in Britain, which makes the survival
of the Manx Electric all the more remarkable. The MER's newest cars (ex-
cepting two replacements in kind for ones lost and one car purchased from
Lisbon) were built in 1906, and the vast majority of the fleet predates 1900.
Nos. 1 and 2, an identical pair delivered in 1893, when the line opened, are
the world's oldest electric cars operating on their original railway—at first
called the Douglas & Laxey Coast Electric Tramway. (Brighton's tiny Volk's
Electric Railway is older, but its surviving cars date from the early years of
the twentieth century.)

Old as they are, the Manx Electric cars shine like new. Just as a pair of trams were ready to leave for Ramsey, we scrambled aboard the open-air trailer—a "toast-rack" car, aptly named for its appearance, with pillars at the ends of each forward-facing bench seat. Riding outside would be invigorating and the best bet for seeing the scenery, so we chose that, but a sign made the parameters of our behavior most explicit: "Warning. Passengers Boarding or Alighting from this Carriage before it has stopped do so at their own risk and contravene the Passenger Transport Act of 1982. It is Dangerous to stand on the Footboard, Lean Out, or Point with the Hand owing the presence of Poles and Structures Close to the Carriage." No problem.

With a "ting-ting" of the motorman's bell, the enclosed "saloon" car ahead—smart in a livery of red, cream, and varnished wood—led us out of town. This pairing of enclosed saloon, handsome with arched windows and angled corner doors, trailing an open car was most typical, although there are powered "toast-racks," and cars do sometimes run singly. Windblown by the brisk morning air, we craned our necks for views of the sea. Groudle was the first reached of the many glens served by the railway; Garwick, Dhoon, Mona, and Ballaglass are others. At Fairy Cottage the line veered inland along Glen Roy to Laxey, where it made a horseshoe bend.

We climbed down at Laxey's nicely restored bungalow-style station and booking office to transfer to the Snaefell Mountain Railway for a 5-mile climb to the summit. (In Manx, similar to Old Norse, *snaefell* means "snow mountain.") This line, with backbreaking grades of 8 percent, was opened in 1895. Nos. 1 through 6, the cars that still serve (though mechanically upgraded in various ways, and with glazing added to their originally open-air windows), were delivered that year. A builder's plate I spotted reading "George F. Milnes & Co. Builders, Tramway & Light Railway Carriage Works, 1895, Birkenhead, England" bore witness. (Milnes also built all the Manx Electric cars delivered before the turn of the last century; the "new" cars, built from 1904 to 1906, came from the United Electric Car Company in Preston, England.)

In spite of their upgrades, the Snaefell cars retain some of their unusual original features. Perhaps the most obvious is the twin "bow collectors" that are used to draw the 550 volts of direct current from the overhead wires. (The earliest cars on the coastal line—now the Manx Electric Railway—also had originally been fitted with bow collectors, but these were replaced with trolley poles in 1897.) The Snaefell line also features a center "Fell" rail, a concept patented in 1863 by John Barraclough Fell, whose son, George Nobel Fell, was the initial surveyor of the Snaefell route. The Fell system placed a raised rail midway between the running rails, providing enhanced adhesion on steam-powered mountain railroads. Although this additional boost wasn't needed on the electrified Snaefell Mountain Railway, the Fell rail provided extra braking as well as enhanced stability to avoid derailments. Presumably the gauge to Snaefell—3½ feet, as opposed to Manx Electric's 3 feet, which prohibits interchange—was chosen to accommodate the Fell gear below the carbody.

"Have you been up the mountain?" our interlocutor aboard the steam railway carriage would ask us later on. "On a real clear day, you can see England, Ireland, Scotland, and Wales from the summit." Couldn't prove it by us. In point of fact, the day we had ridden, our car had begun its upgrade grind from Laxey bathed in warm sun. To our right, the 72½-foot-tall, red-spoked Laxey Wheel churned ponderously. Now a tourist attraction (it's said to be the largest functioning waterwheel in the world), it once pumped water from the area's lead mines. Soon enough, however, we'd ascended into clouds. Mist billowed in the open windows like smoke. At the frigid, dank summit, we inhabited a closed-in, gray-white world. At Summit Station, in the Snaefell Mountain Café—"the island's top café," it boasted, without fear of contradiction—we ordered steaming coffee with hot milk, then happily boarded our car to descend back into summer.

Before continuing our journey to Ramsey, we lunched at Mines Tavern (formerly the Station Hotel) at Laxey, which sported CAMRA credentials. (The Campaign for Real Ale supports local, hand-pulled, cask-conditioned brews.) Although the bar was designed to suggest a MER saloon car, we chose the garden, where we could watch Manx Electric and Snaefell Mountain trams shuttle by while we ate "baps"—sandwich rolls—and quaffed Bushy's Manx Bitter. "Take a tram to the ale of Man," read the bar coasters at Mines Tavern, and that's exactly what we'd done.

Later, as the afternoon waned, we headed north once more, on to Ramsey. The terrain en route featured rocky cliffs that fell straight down to the sea. Their starkness was relieved by rolling hills, with flocks of grazing sheep showing white against the green. Once or twice the trams screeched to a stop at a remote "halt," or station, then clanged ahead again, rattling and rolling comfortably. All in all, it was a gentle, bucolic journey of seascapes and pastures, which we spun in reverse as soon as we reached our destination.

Then, returning through Laxey, we found the No. 2. This car, which had an open motorman's platform and a 110-yar history, we knew we had to ride. Waiting for No. 2, running as an unscheduled "extra" train, to depart, we chatted with Dave, the motorman, who had worked for Manx Electric in the 1970s and recently returned on a seasonal basis.

"Once, at a trolley museum in California," he said, "I told the volunteers that I was a motorman. They kept referring to 'your museum.' They couldn't get it through their heads that this wasn't a museum, just a railroad that lasted." And last it should continue to do, we figured, since—like the steam railway, the Snaefell Mountain, and the horse trams—it was now owned and operated

A horse tram on the seaside Promenade at Douglas.

by Isle of Man Transport, a government agency. These railways were clearly a draw for tourists, who now visit the island in much reduced numbers.

"Tourism today represents less than 5 percent of the island's GNP," Dave said. "It's a ghost of what it was 30 years ago." Inexpensive flights to sunnier climes clearly have diverted many holiday-making Brits. But No. 2, which we did ride back to Douglas, soldiers on as bravely as ever. Rich, Laurel, and I each had a turn outside on the motorman's platform with Dave, as he swung the controller through the notches to urge the car along the curvy, up-and-down line. "Even in bad weather, I like the fresh air," he said. "But a sunny afternoon like this is perfect." Inside, the varnished longitudinal bench seats "worked" against my back as the wooden car flexed. Everything creaked, and the windows danced in their frames.

We passed the stop for Groudle Glen, where we would return in the evening to ride the excursion railway there. As we dropped down into Douglas on the Manx Electric car, I saw the inbound *Ben-My-Chree* headed for the North Quay. This vehicle ferry—its name means "girl of my heart"—would be our departing transportation; though inelegantly top-heavy, at least it was a real ship, but no match for the earlier, graceful *Manxman, Manx Maid,* or the even more ancient and elegant *Lady of Mann.*

Leaving Dave to return No. 2 to the car barn after yet another day's productive work, we climbed aboard a horse tram to ride the length of the seaside Promenade at a steady clip-clop. This 20-minute trip showed off the often-exceptional Victorian architecture of downtown to good advantage, including the brilliantly restored Gaiety Theater of 1899. By the time it was built, the horse trams had been running for 23 years. We spotted the Empress Hotel, where Laurel and I had stayed in 1970, still looking good. In contrast, the Hilton Hotel and Casino was a brutal chunk of concrete. The horse trams were open-air, toast-rack cars, in service since the line's opening. The conductor swung acrobatically along the running board to collect fares—two pounds for a round-trip. At the terminus, he and the driver walked the horse around to the other end of the car. They flipped over the seats, and the tram was set to depart again, ready to carry another load of riders down the block and back in time.

Back in time is also where we went that evening, when we hopped a Manx Electric saloon car for the short trip to Groudle Glen and the railway there. Tiny even by Manx standards—2-foot-gauge, rather than 3-foot, like the Manx Electric and the steam railway, and only a mile long—the Groudle Glen Railway dates from the era when Groudle was a resort and amusement center sporting an open-air dance floor and seaside zoo with sea lions and polar bears. The aptly named *Sea Lion,* the diminutive 2-4-0T steam locomotive that would haul our tiny train, had been on hand for the line's opening in 1896.

R. M. Broadbent, the railway's developer and owner, had trouble finding a builder for so tiny a locomotive, but Bagnalls, Ltd., of Stafford eventually came through with a side-tank engine a mere 12 feet long. A decade later, in 1906, business would warrant a second, similar locomotive, which would be named *Polar Bear.* It survives as well and has made guest appearances back in the Glen. When the Groudle Glen line opened, it was advertised as "the Smallest Passenger Railway in the World." *Locomotive Magazine* deemed it the first miniature railway with open cars for public pleasure riding.

In 1894 Broadbent had opened the Groudle Hotel at the head of the glen, alongside the new Manx Electric. One hundred and nine years later we would walk through the gathering darkness of that woody glen on the path Broadbent had built, past ferny pools and waterfalls to the train shed at Lhen Coan—"lonely valley" in Manx. The feeling was a trifle ghostly, appropriate for a now-empty place where years ago the laughter of merrymakers echoed—and for a railway that had already died once. Faltering after World

Sea Lion at the Lhen Coan terminal of the Groudle Glen Railway.

War II, the line had shut down completely in 1962, and all the rails had been lifted through the late 1960s.

By 1982, when restoration of the railroad began, it had virtually vanished without a trace. Volunteers re-laid the track, reaching the end of the line at Sea Lion Rocks in 1992, and replicated the canopy building at Lhen Coan. From there we would chuff out into the low evening sun, out to Sea Lion Rocks, where crowds once visited the zoo. We found nothing but a breezy, sun-swept seascape, a reconstructed station, and the rocky cove once artificially enclosed to hold the performing sea lions.

When, two days later, we steamed away on *Ben-My-Chree* and watched Douglas Head vanish into the mist, we each had some regrets about our too-brief visit. Rich wished we'd hiked up to the great waterwheel at Laxey, and Laurel wished that we'd dined at Café Tanroagan, an attractive little restaurant that we'd discovered only after dinner on our last evening.

And my regret? That we had to let this magical Brigadoon slide back into slumber. But, I reasoned, I'd most likely be able to awaken it again in the future just by showing up and boarding a train or tram.

Another Seaside Electric Railway

The Manx Electric Railway is ancient, small, and—being Manx—somewhat eccentric. However, it's not the oldest, narrowest, shortest, oddest electric railway in the British Isles. For that honor, I nominate Volk's Electric Railway in Brighton, a classic blue-collar English seaside resort not unlike the Isle of Man. It's located on England's south coast, and in April 2007 Laurel and I headed there from nearby Southampton, where we'd disembarked from Celebrity Cruises' *Constellation* after a "repositioning" voyage across the Atlantic.

Like the Isle of Man, the city surely had lost some of its luster since cheap vacation packages to warmer places became available, but Brighton Rock, the iconic hard candy that gave novelist Graham Greene a title for one of his thrillers, is still on offer. There's a bustling railway station dating from 1840 with as fine a train shed as any medium-size British city could hope for. However, it wasn't any of the mainline services that

radiated from that stub-end terminal that most caught my fancy. Rather, it was Volk's Electric Railway.

To locate this anomalous railway, I first found Brighton Pier, a 1,722-foot-long finger poking into the English Channel. Opened in 1899 and called Palace Pier for much of its life, it looks like a horizontal Victorian wedding cake. It was Chain Pier, an older structure on that site, that Volk's first served when it opened in 1883. Volk's is the oldest operating electric railway in the world and was Britain's first electric line. Except for a few years during World War II, it has never been closed.

When I arrived at the Aquarium Station, near the pier, Car No. 9 was just rolling in with Dave Cowstick at the controller. Waiting to board, I learned from him that his 40-seat open car dated from 1910; that the line had been built in 2-foot gauge but was quickly converted to 2 feet 8½ inches; that the cars run on 110-volt D.C., transmitted through a third rail. I boarded, and off the car rattled on its roughly 1.25-mile route along the beach. At Half Way Point, the location of the line's modest car shed, we met cars No. 7 and 8 (built in 1901) headed back to Aquarium from the far end of the line, Black Rock Station.

Waiting for time at Black Rock before my own return, Cowstick told me about the line's founder, Magnus Volk, born in Brighton in 1851, the son of a clockmaker. Electricity was in its infancy when Volk reached adulthood, and it became his passion. His was the first house in Brighton equipped with electric lights and telephone. He then received the commission to electrify Brighton's astonishing, India-influenced Royal Pavilion, built for George IV when he was Prince Regent. This project was completed in 1883, the year Volk opened his railway. Although it had been relocated in places and trimmed a bit, I found the railway looking and running much as it did on May 7, 1937, when the 85-year-old Volk took the controls of Car No. 10 to celebrate the opening of a new station building at Black Rock. Volk died peacefully in his sleep just 13 days later, but his railway lives on.

The ancient cars of Volk's Electric Railway ply the Brighton beachfront.

At El Matién on the Esquel Branch in Patagonia.

BIBLIOGRAPHY

Eagleson, Mike. "The 2-10-4's of Tubarão." *Railfan & Railroad* 2 (September 1979):

Edwards, Barry. *The Manx Electric Railway.* Ickenham, Middlesex: B&C
  Publications, 1998.

Johnson, Eric L. *The Sea-to-Sky Gold Rush Route.* Vancouver: Rusty Spike, 1998.

Mulvihill, C. E. *White Pass & Yukon Route Handbook.* Oakland: R. Robb, 2000.

Nazarow, Greg. "It's a 'Krok'!" *Railfan & Railroad* 8 (June 1989): 54–60.

Rainey, Lee, and Frank Kyper. *East Broad Top.* San Marino, Calif.: Golden
  West Books, 1982.

Sepiurka, Sergio Daniel, and Jorge Alberto Miglioli. *La Trochita: A Journey
  through Time and Distance on the Old Patagonian Express.* Buenos Aires:
  Grupo Abierto Comunicaciones, 2001.

Clock and flowers in Alexisbad on the Harz
Mountain Narrow Gauge Railways.

INDEX

Photo courtesy of Laurel Zimmermann

KARL ZIMMERMANN is the author or coauthor of 22 books, including *CZ: The Story of the California Zephyr, Santa Fe Streamliners: The Chiefs and Their Tribesmen, Magnetic North: Canadian Steam in Twilight, 20th Century Limited, Burlington's Zephyrs,* and *The GrandLuxe Express: Traveling in High Style.* An accomplished writer and photographer whose love of trains has sparked a lifetime of travel worldwide, Zimmermann has been a frequent contributor to the travel sections of newspapers across the country, including the *New York Times, Los Angeles Times,* and *Washington Post,* while his stories and photographs have been published in numerous magazines, including *Trains, Classic Trains, Railfan & Railroad,* and *Passenger Train Journal.*